Finally, a refreshing approach to growing a business that offers clear direction and simple, well-thought-out res~~ources~~ ~~A wonderful~~ *story of adventure tied with great insight into*

—Ryan de Milliano, C.E.T., Owner | RAD Media

Freezing My Ass Off on Kilimanjaro is a compelling read and "script" for entrepreneurs and anyone with a penchant for creating value. Leanne Brownoff has deep experience in helping businesses understand and execute the daunting route needed for a successful summit. And she makes her knowledge wonderfully accessible as she connects it to an actual climb up Kilimanjaro. Brownoff leverages this perfect analogy and, as she does, novice and seasoned business leaders will find the book both entertaining and informative. Buy it, read it, and put it to work for your own climb.

—Lorne Rubis , Chief Evangelist ATB Financial
Author, *The Character Triangle*

Maybe it's not even fair to call Kilimanjaro *solely a book. It's a business strategy, expert advice, and inspiring metaphor in one. The A.C.T.I.O.N. Plan is an accessible strategy any entrepreneur, team leader, or business owner can use at any stage of business. With plain language and clear questions to ask of yourself, it allows the reader to easily identify where you are in the stages, what's going right, and where and when you need to pivot.* Kilimanjaro *creates a challenge to other writers of business books equal to that of the mountain's impressive peaks. How will they accomplish nearly as much as Leanne Brownoff manages to pack into this book?*

—Jeff Samsonow, Publisher at Edmonton Quotient,
Producer of Media and Television

This book is a defined road map to success and an insight into where you want your life, your vision to be. Definitely on the reading list for all entrepreneurs!

—Gay Derk, President of Derks & Bridal
Fantasy, Bridal Fantasy Magazine

Freezing
My Ass Off
on Kilimanjaro

The entrepreneur's survival guide for building traction on a changing business terrain

Leanne Brownoff

ISBN-13: 978-1-7751005-08

Editing, interior design, and production by Joanne Shwed, Backspace Ink (www.backspaceink.com)

Frosted background design and cover consultant: Tikina Gordey
Front cover graphic: Leanne Brownoff
Cover design: Joanne Shwed, Leanne Brownoff
Back cover photo: Ryan de Milliano, RAD Media
Audio sound mixing: Chris "Hollywood" Holmes
Music written and performed by Nick Brownoff

Photo credits: "Kilimanjaro" (page 6), "Ha Ling" (page 32), and "Sunrise from Uhuru" (page 189) by Leanne Brownoff. "Mawenzi" (page 52) and "Zebra Rock" (page 98) by Jessica Brownoff. "Mandara Hut" (page 144) by Cameron Taylor. "Uhuru Summit" (page 170) by Joe Munuo.

To my wonderful family:

To my husband Larry, who graciously supported me through the original experiences that started the A.C.T.I.O.N. Plan as well as the challenges I experienced while creating this book.

To my son Nicholas, whose calm wisdom inspires me to see past the known and imagine the possibilities.

To my son Christopher, who inspires me to take on challenges and stare down fears.

To my daughter Jessica, who has been my constant supporter and action companion, from helping me through technical challenges to standing on top of the world with me.

You are the most action-oriented people I know. You inspire me every day to go that extra mile to make a difference.

Mount Kilimanjaro, Tanzania, Africa—the world's tallest freestanding mountain (5,895 meters/19,341 feet)

In life and in business, achieving success starts with a vision. To stand on that summit, you need the ability to visualize that success and follow a process that will guide you through uncertain terrain, which builds traction when you become frozen or stuck along the way.

" Never let fear determine your goals.
If fear of the unknown keeps you doing
The same things,
The same way
All the time—
You are going to create a rut that's
too deep to get out of. "

Contents

Foreword

The A.C.T.I.O.N. Plan is a process that almost jumped out and presented itself to me. Over the years, I have developed it and honed it, not just for myself but also for my clients. Ever since I can remember, like most people, I have been presented with obstacles in my eclectic and varied career. I started with a large pharmaceutical company whose senior management had decided that I was not qualified for the sales position I had applied for. In fact, I was called "a skirt in a man's world" and told that I would be "chewed up and spit out" in that world.

I have always attributed my feisty drive to my Irish father and Polish mother. But, in the moment of sink or swim, I chose to swim—or at least to tread water. The exhausting interview resulted in a tentative nod for me to proceed. It was a perplexing feeling. On one hand, I was relieved to get the job because the economy at the time was depressed, and my husband and I had a mortgage with a hefty interest rate; on the other, I could feel waves of doubt flooding over me like breakers hitting a beach during the hurricane season. It occurred to me that I had just fought for and accepted a position with a company that had no belief in me; in fact, the last words I heard in that interview were, "You will probably be a waste of time and money, and I doubt if you will make it past training."

This was just the beginning of a long list of trials I experienced with this position. I soon found out that my newly acquired territory in the company I had just joined was a distant third (out of three major brands). I did not have the support of the head office, and I was selling a brand that no one was buying. Although there was a lofty sales target expected, there were no strategies offered to achieve them.

Many people who have heard the complete version of this story have said, "I would have left on the spot."

However, as challenging as this first step into the business world was for me, I hold the experience tightly to my heart and am so grateful I had it. You see, even though all odds were against me, I wasn't willing to quit just because it seemed hard. I decided that what I did with this situation was completely up to me. I needed to prove—not so much to them but to me—that I could take this challenge and create an opportunity. I wanted to meet their target and exceed it.

I made it past my three-month probation and, at the annual year-end national convention, I was awarded for top sales performance of the year. I attained my target *and* exceeded it by 10%. What was more important to me than winning an award was the fact that I had assisted my colleagues, and they had banner years as well. Remember: When I signed on, we were a distant third; after my first year with the company, everything changed. I was asked by the corporate head office to lead a national training program, teaching teams across the country about my success.

Their definitive yet ambiguous directive stated, "Just tell them what you do."

Tell them what I do? I thought. *I just do what I do.*

At that time, the first stages of what would become the A.C.T.I.O.N. Plan began to emerge. The national training program started with the most challenging territories. Like my experience, the teams were faced with abysmal sales. After thinking about how to develop a process that could be easily shared with others yet flexible enough to adjust to individual needs, I began to craft a procedure that reflected my methods. For many of my colleagues, this was the first time that any form of a strategy was introduced in their business.

Although the process was originally created in a sales atmosphere, it became apparent to me that it was relevant for all forms and at all levels of business. I believe success isn't something that occurs by happenstance. It transpires from a carefully crafted plan built on constant awareness. It requires flexibility to maneuver challenges, embraces a willingness to learn from others, and offers a celebration in the spirit of gratitude. This plan was applicable for winning contracts and market share. It also allowed people to be engaged fully in a process that enabled them to understand the results they were getting and to proactively make adjustments in an ever-changing world in order to focus on their targets. It offered a process that allowed their passion to be rekindled and, with that, resulted in growing enthusiasm for creating opportunities.

When I left two and one-half years later, the company was solidly in the #1 spot nationally. I did not single-handedly make this happen, but I did start the ripple that had far-reaching consequences. I had taken the challenge and found a way up the mountain.

Over the years, I have worked for and with some amazingly brilliant men and women. In each case, they echoed that first directive: "Can you teach my team what you do?" This request soon evolved into working directly with key decision makers in international companies, consulting with the C-suite in businesses, and mentoring medium- to small-sized businesses. The process is applicable to all levels of an organization; however, if the company's decision makers and visionaries do not embrace it first, it will have limited impact.

The approach I bring to my clients today is based on that original process, and I am sharing it with you in this book. I have developed the A.C.T.I.O.N. Plan to provide a base on which to build your business or to move it to the next level. It is as applicable for someone with an idea sketched on a napkin as it is for a business owner who has years of experience but is not sure how to move the business forward. This tool can assist a company to maneuver during turbulent times as well as offer a plan for expansion. It is applicable to every stage of a business—from embryo to exit.

Originally, the A.C.T.I.O.N. Plan was created in an audio format. I wanted people to have this tool at their fingertips, in their office, while in transit, or out for a run. My experience with adult learning prompted me to develop a workbook to augment the audio message, allowing people to work on their own projects as they went through each phase. The workbook soon evolved into a full book with the ability to scan the audio segments. This format allows you to experience the process in many ways, improving recall and building on traction. You'll note that audio segments refer to CDs, which were the original format intent; however, they have now been integrated into the chapters of the book for your convenience.

The book and audio segments are filled with inspirational thoughts to help you stay focused on the goal and to move you through the process. Even though this book speaks specifically to business goals, I soon found that it is applicable to almost any goal—business or personal—that you set for yourself.

My daughter Jessica and I had an amazing experience climbing Mount Kilimanjaro in Tanzania, Africa, and I used the A.C.T.I.O.N. Plan process for the entire experience. The challenges were definitely present, particularly on the last six hours of our climb. Under the light of a super moon, our team of four started the last six-hour leg of our summit at midnight, at the mercy of our trained guides. As they led us up the steep and rocky terrain, reaching the altitude of 5,895 meters/19,341 feet, the cold temperatures froze our water supply and left our hands and feet numb. The slow and mesmerizing steps put my mind in a trance and, through a series of dreamlike flashbacks, I began to recall the initial seed of the idea my friend Kathy and I had planted—from awareness to commitment, to finding our team, to implementing our plan, to experiencing amazing opportunities, to finally taking the ultimate step that placed me on top of the highest freestanding mountain in the world.

While we watched the sunrise on the vast horizon, we realized that we had succeeded at something truly amazing. Upon our descent, our thoughts were focused on what was next.

This A.C.T.I.O.N. Plan process is set with the Kilimanjaro experience as a metaphorical backdrop for business. Each chapter begins with excerpts from the climb, which are then translated into the business processes you can use in your personal climb. It is my intent that you experience passion and success in the goals you set for yourself. This is not a quick fix or a fast track to the finish line. It is, however, a process that can guide your decisions and help you maneuver the challenges you will face, so that you too can summit your mountain.

Leanne Brownoff
Business Consultant

Acknowledgments

Larry, my husband and sounding board: Thank you for keeping me in "Implementation" mode.

Nicholas, my son and creative musician: Thank you for your endless patience and amazing musical contribution. Music makes everything better.

Christopher, my son and steady wave of support: Thank you for your artistic inspiration and your stellar and calming words of wisdom.

Jessica, my daughter and right (and left) hand: Thank you for being my sounding board, tech support, and social media teacher. Thank you for summiting Kilimanjaro with me—an amazing A.C.T.I.O.N. experience.

Tikina Gordey: Thank you for your creative solutions that built traction to overcome stubborn technical challenges. Your tenacity to solve a problem, regardless of how busy you are, is greatly appreciated.

Joanne Shwed of Backspace Ink: Thanks for your guidance and patience in moving the process along, particularly in my lengthy communication gaps.

Chris "Hollywood" Holmes: Thanks for sound mixing and mastering.

Catalin Negraru and Anum Usman: Thanks for being my tech problem solvers and audio link creators.

Kathy Matear: Thanks for being an inspiring friend and a role model businesswoman and for experiencing Kilimanjaro with me. I will always look at obstacles differently now.

Cameron Taylor: Thanks for being my Kilimanjaro teammate, who moved through obstacles like a gazelle, proving action makes traction.

Good Earth Tours: Thanks for providing an inspiring metaphor for the A.C.T.I.O.N. Plan.

Our entire Kilimanjaro team of guides and porters: Thanks for exemplifying how critical teamwork is in successfully accomplishing your goals.

Rob Petkau, a true, modern-day Jedi: The "force" is always with you. Thanks for the many coffee meetings where your wise words put business and life conundrums into perspective and for sharing your valuable insight for this project with the audience.

Dr. Deborah Nixon, PhD: Thanks for your passion and commitment to building business relationships and trust and for your refreshing perspective on creating opportunities. Our many conversations will always be treasured. You are truly an action-oriented woman who inspires many.

Dale Monaghan: Thanks for your generous spirit and engaging personality that inspire businesses to look beyond limitations and redefine what a successful team is.

Dianna Bowes: Thanks for your generous entrepreneurial spirit and contagious verve for life. Your ripple in life and in business is great, and you continue to be an inspiration for business owners now and in the future.

Maureen Wright, the Mo of MoJo: Thank you for sharing your entrepreneurial story with our audience. Your vision is far reaching and an inspiration to others who have dreams.

Johanne Lewis, the Jo of MoJo: Thank you for your fearless energy and for sharing your experiences with our audience. Your unwavering tenacity is a gift I wish for all business owners. The MoJo story is a great lesson about working hard, working smart, never giving up, and having fun doing it all.

Carol Aubee Girard: You are a generous spirit and a role-model businesswoman who proves that you can be in the C-suite, be a supportive marriage partner, raise a fine family, and still have time to volunteer in the community. Thank you for your contribution to this project and for being such an amazing friend.

Elaine Sadler and ATB Financial: Thanks for your constant support as a business sounding board. Our seminars proved that there is a need to reach out and encourage smart business practice for entrepreneurs.

Dr. Michelle Cleveland, a relentless warrior and intelligent businesswoman: You exemplify the belief that personal health is the cornerstone to business and personal success. Thank you for your many contributions to this project.

Cheryl Joseph: Thank you for your unwavering belief in this project and assisting in the journey that made traction.

Cynthia Pratt: Thanks for your ability to display grace under pressure. You were my lifeboat during 9/11 and an inspiration to anyone facing challenges. Thank you for being my sounding board for this project.

And finally my many clients: You have been my inspiration to hone and develop this process. Your tenacity to lead your given industries has inspired me to reach further. You have taken the process of the A.C.T.I.O.N. Plan and personalized it to be relevant to your individual needs. Thank you for your enthusiasm to choose action over mediocrity.

Introduction

What's in a title? Well, this title got you curious enough to get to this page, so, in some measure, it has been successful. The title started from a collaboration of ideas on which this book is based. The ultimate point of the book is to share the critical phases that I have successfully imparted into business organizations. At times, the businesses are at the embryonic stages, and sometimes they are well established but literally frozen. In my personal climb of Mount Kilimanjaro—the world's tallest freestanding mountain—I was constantly reminded of the similarities that the climb of the mountain had to the climb of a business. I knew the book would present the stages of the climb as a backdrop to the business process I was sharing, but I drew a blank when it was time to create the title of the book.

Fortunately, I choose to surround myself with highly creative and curious people. Curious people always find innovative ways of seeing problems and coming up with intriguing solutions. One such moment occurred during a business meeting with Kyle Loranger, a witty and highly creative graphic/web designer (owner of Kyle Loranger Design Inc.). Our conversation moved to my book progress—in particular, the title. After sharing a few of my thoughts, he slowly and methodically pulled away from the table (a sign that the creativity was flowing).

Teetering on the back legs of his chair, he stared past me through the window of his office. He slowly settled the front legs of his chair back on the floor and looked at me with a Cheshire grin.

"You know what popped into my head?" he asked. "*Freezing My Ass Off on Kilimanjaro!*"

I stared back, not sure if he was serious. But he was, and he had an explanation to back it:

"As small business owners and entrepreneurs, we are all at some point painfully struggling. We are, metaphorically, out on a limb, hanging on a cliff, or freezing in the wilderness. We get stuck … frozen. We're here, but we want to go there," he said, pointing his finger to the ceiling. "Then you come and offer that lifeline, which takes us to where we want to be. You literally froze your ass off on Kilimanjaro. But, for us, it's a metaphor. You just can't sugar coat it. Running a successful business is scary and hard!"

I smiled as I realized that I had found the missing puzzle piece. Kyle had recognized the value in the process and connected the dots for other entrepreneurs in a real way.

I had chosen Kilimanjaro for a reason. It represents a big challenge, which is the same as making a business successful. The title had to speak to the real challenges of running a business.

And so it was decided. The book would be titled, *Freezing My Ass Off on Kilimanjaro.*

Welcome to the A.C.T.I.O.N. Plan

Y ou are about to be introduced to a business success strategy that will provide you with keys on which to build a strong foundation. The A.C.T.I.O.N. Plan consists of six integral stages of development, which can apply to any business regardless of its scope and size: (1) Awareness; (2) Commitment; (3) Team; (4) Implementation; (5) Opportunities; and (6) Next.

This six-part plan is designed specifically for the businessperson who doesn't settle for good but strives for exceptional. It is for the creative entrepreneur who is motivated by the mantra, "Why not?" It is for the strategic thinker who recognizes that success follows a carefully crafted plan.

To amplify your learning experience, this book has been created in conjunction with an audio series (see "A.C.T.I.O.N. Plan Introduction" on page 30 as an example). The audio links will allow you to continuously learn while you are "on the go." Whether you are commuting, working out at the gym, or enjoying a run or hike, the audio series will follow the six steps to support business success. Each format offers additional information that builds from the other to provide a greater scope to each topic, using an engaging and memorable process. The book offers charts, graphs, and forms that will be useful as you move your business from good to great. The audio series also includes valuable advice from successful businesspeople who know how critical these steps are for developing strong and sustainable businesses.

In all business ventures, it is important to know who your target audience is and who it is not. Although this information can benefit anyone in business, it is specifically intended for:

- The individual who is considering starting up a business
- The individual who currently owns a business but needs to build traction to see greater results
- The individual who is interested in expanding their current business

- The individual who has not thought of an exit strategy or a succession plan
- The individual who has an entrepreneurial spirit but is currently in an unfulfilling position
- The serious business-minded individual who has a track record of success in other areas of their life but has yet to be passionate about their daily business
- The individual who feels like they are stuck in neutral and has a great desire to switch gears but doesn't know how

Finally, this program is intended for:

- The individual who enjoys learning new approaches and who wants their legacy to be as a leader whose footsteps are worth following

You will soon appreciate that the six steps begin to move in sync, like the interlocking gears of a well-oiled machine. As your experiences begin to shape your personal success strategy, the meaning behind the word "action" becomes evident.

This series challenges the concept of simply "going with the flow." It challenges the fear that paralyzes us from venturing forth to pursue a life we want to experience. Regardless of the size of your business or where it is in its life cycle, it is imperative that you possess the mindset that refuses to accept mediocrity.

The following is my mantra, which I live by and which was the impetus for this plan:

" Don't be a spectator in your own life.
You were intended to play the leading role.
Do it with passion! "

When you take responsibility for your life and its results, you feel and act differently. Your actions have a purpose because you are invested in the outcome. Stalling in the face of an obstacle is natural, but always succumbing to a retreat without evaluating your options can result in a deep rut.

When you perpetuate the same actions and thoughts, you engrave the experience into your mind, and soon you believe that there are no other options than the situations that continuously present themselves to you.

Much of our challenge in life and in business is based on fear and, to a great degree, we allow the fear to lead our destiny. The A.C.T.I.O.N. Plan will allow you to consider what you want to achieve and what—if anything—may be holding you back. It will guide you to understand how you react to situations and offer steps you can take to move through the process.

The obvious and most fundamental aspect of succeeding in business and in life is to keep moving!

A.C.T.I.O.N. Plan Introduction

https://goo.gl/u7t9cE
(time 12:59)

Using a scan app, scan the QR code above, or use
the above link to access the sound file.

Note: Please allow a few moments for the file to open on your device.

A.C.T.I.O.N. PLAN

CHAPTER 1

Awareness

View of Ha Ling Peak, part of the majestic Rocky Mountains.

At some point all successful people question the path they are on.
In order to gain critical perspective, they know they
must step out of ruts and create a new path.

Lessons from the Mountain ...

The idea of climbing Kilimanjaro came from an auspicious "girls' weekend" surrounded by the glorious Rocky Mountains. I was connecting with a long-time friend. Kathy and I went way back to junior high school days. We had spent long summers volunteering with aboriginal communities in northern Alberta, had served on the school council, and can even say that we toured in a singing group. (Okay, so it was a high school singing group called PITCH and SPICE. Although you likely haven't heard of it, those experiences became some of my best memories, which I used to build on years later.)

Kathy and I had the kind of friendship where we could be out of contact for years, and then pick up where we left off without missing a beat. Our career paths followed a business focus; her path, however, had allowed her to travel the world. I had traveled to Europe, the Pacific, and a great deal of North America. She had traveled to every continent many times.

After enjoying a magnificent meal prepared by Kathy, we relaxed by a roaring fire. Feet up on a hassock, wrapped in cozy quilts to stave off the February chill.

Kathy had just refilled my wine glass—again—when I asked her, "What place would you like to travel to that you haven't been to yet?"

Without hesitation, she said, "I would love to climb Kilimanjaro." Kathy had already made plans to trek through the Rwandan jungles to view the amazing gorillas and had been thinking about Kilimanjaro.

"Wouldn't that be amazing?" I asked. "I have never been to Africa, and Kilimanjaro has always been on my bucket list."

"Let's do it!" said Kathy enthusiastically. "Let's climb Kilimanjaro!"

I realized this was moving to a more serious discussion. "When?"

"Why not this summer?"

"Perfect!" I said, riding on the excitement of the idea.

The next morning found us snowshoeing, a little sluggishly for me (thanks to the wine), through pristine fields of glistening, white snow, maneuvering

A.C.T.I.O.N. PLAN

the deep banks that had crested from the previous night's wind. The air was crisp and fresh as miniature ice crystals hung in the air. It was a perfect morning (except for the heavy head).

"So," Kathy started hesitantly, "you were serious about Kilimanjaro, weren't you?"

Now, in the clarity of day, the exciting idea started to get weighed down with questions:

"How can I get away to do a trip like that?"

"What about my business and my family?"

"How much will this cost?"

"How high is this mountain?"

"Is it dangerous? What is the success rate of the climbers?"

"Am I fit enough? If not, do I need to start training?"

"How do you even go about planning for a trip like this?"

Like so many great ideas, this one was teetering on the brink of falling back into the bucket. Unfettered conversations that resulted in napkin sketches or mastermind thoughts that were ignited by a line in a movie are familiar moments to many. But, when viewed through the lens of doubt, the napkin gets crumpled and taken away with the remains of your meal, or the credits roll and the exiting crowds remind you that you are in a sea of ideas. Why would yours work?

I had noticed over the years that, given the right set of circumstances, people could come up with great ideas but they struggled with the commitment and execution of them. Committing to something that makes you stretch beyond your comfort level is a real deal breaker for many people. In business, many ideas barely get launched because of fear: fear of failure, fear of making a costly decision, and fear of—well, frankly—looking stupid. Nobody wants to be remembered for having a failure to shoulder for eternity.

Then, realizing that I hadn't answered Kathy, I said, "Hell, yeah!"

A.C.T.I.O.N. PLAN

You see, I knew that the questions swirling in my head were important ones, and they needed to be addressed—not ignored. But that was simply part of the awareness phase of taking on this challenge.

My answer of "Hell, yeah!" was very real and very true. I was serious about Kilimanjaro. Now was the time to ask more questions in order to get the answers that would build greater awareness. This would be a critical phase of discovery. Thinking about the end goal was both exhilarating and scary, not unlike a new innovative idea or business opportunity, whether conceived on a napkin or presented in a boardroom.

The first part of my awareness was to make a list of questions. Not just the ones that had flooded my brain that morning when the crisp, cool, mountain air plunged me back to reality. No, I needed to step back and see the big picture.

Having a goal is one thing, but making it happen successfully requires a plan. In order to create that plan, I would need to do some research.

I have always taken a scientific approach to business and problem solving. In my early years at university, the science classes resonated with me. We were trained to question everything from a place of facts. We understood that repeating the same experiment often gave the same results, which were great for understanding technique but not for uncovering new ideas. When an experiment did not turn out the way you had expected, my lab teaching assistants were excited because it presented a real learning opportunity. We weren't chastised for the unexpected result if we could explain why it happened and how that chance occurrence could be useful in the future. The world was presented in terms of possibilities not yet experienced, and I took that lens with me to the business world.

Business is in many ways like a science experiment. The parts of an experiment include a purpose, a hypothesis, the experiment, an analysis, and a conclusion. As you will see, the phases of the A.C.T.I.O.N. Plan mirror these steps. You will also see how the Kilimanjaro trek also parallels the steps

A.C.T.I.O.N. PLAN

presented, suggesting that, with the correct process in place, you can reach your goals and reach new heights.

How to Create Awareness in Your Business

Awareness is a dynamic state of perception. It engages all senses in combination with knowledge, experience, and beliefs. Our awareness can be dulled when routines become numbing; conversely, they can be heightened when contrasting options are presented. There are signs around us every minute of every day that we often miss because we are engrained in a routine. In effect, we go through life with blinders on, which can derail our efforts to be successful.

Awareness is a living stage where data are constantly being presented, evaluated, and stored in our experiential database, which defines our perception of the facts. This ongoing knowledge collection is ready for our use given our situations. As you proceed through this chapter, you will be introduced to exercises that will assist you in:

- Thinking in possibilities to awaken your personal and business goals;
- Evaluating what you bring to the process; and
- Understanding what you need to acquire in order to experience success.

Position yourself in the realm of possibilities, not limitations. Remove all distractions to focus on the big picture, not the next fire that is about to run through your door. If you struggle to remove yourself mentally from your daily routine, schedule some time physically away from it (e.g., an hour, a day, a weekend, or whatever time you need) to solidify this initial step.

A.C.T.I.O.N. PLAN

The Awareness stage encourages you to gather facts about yourself, your business (or business idea), and the world around you in order to understand how that knowledge can help your business succeed.

Identify Critical Points for Your Business

We often hear people say, "It's business; it's not personal," but strategically positioning yourself for success in business is personal … *very* personal. In this section, we will discuss some critical points that require you to stop and evaluate how prepared you are for the future.

The chart entitled "Your Personal Awareness Questionnaire" on page 39 presents questions to help you evaluate yourself on 10 critical points. The first two questions deal with health. Everyone in business knows that you can only ignore your health for so long before something forces you to pay attention to it. My business and personal goals are rooted in being proactive, learning as much as I can to make decisions and plans that provide me with options, not limitations. Keeping an eye on your health is a way to ensure that you maximize your potential. If you are healthy, you will make better decisions and not be preoccupied with physical annoyances, which can plague the most focused entrepreneur. With professional guidance, you can take precautionary or corrective steps to live a healthy life.

The sad reality is that we often get so busy that we take our health for granted. We are to a great extent the saboteurs of our own success. You may blame other people or circumstances for things not going in the direction you want; however, we will see the biggest culprit looking back in our mirror.

Here's my challenge to you if you truly want to be successful: Take responsibility for your life! This starts with your health. Your health is the

You have to know what you are taking into the arena before you can expect to win the match.

foundation that will support your ideas and provide the stamina you will need for the road ahead.

"Your Personal Awareness Questionnaire" will provide a reference point as to how you view your readiness to pursue your business goals. Be as honest as possible. This is intended to be a first evaluation. As you progress through the phases, your awareness will become greater, and you will likely make adjustments that will move up your personal ratings. It will only take a few minutes, but it will start you thinking. As you proceed through the six phases of the A.C.T.I.O.N. Plan, come back to this questionnaire and compare how your responses have changed.

Get to Know Yourself ... Again!

Your Personal Awareness Questionnaire

Please indicate your level of satisfaction for each question presented, using a scale of 1 to 10 (1 is low satisfaction and 10 is high satisfaction).

AWARENESS POINTS	SCORE
General health	
Physical stamina	
Ability to set goals	
Ability to delegate	
Ability to achieve business goals	
Ability to achieve financial goals	
Ability to achieve personal goals	
Time management (balancing demands)	
Confidence level to achieve success	
Happiness and career satisfaction	
Total Score: _____%	

The results of this questionnaire do not offer scientific value as every answer is based on your perception. This is a reflective exercise that requires you to place a value on each personal criterion. These points have initiated the process of personal awareness. Regardless of where you rate yourself on the satisfaction continuum, the A.C.T.I.O.N. Plan will challenge you to strive for a new level of success. When you look back at your answers, reflect on what caused you to respond in the manner that you did.

Curiosity is a gift we are born with, but we lose it when we opt for safe paths. It's good to be cautious but invaluable to be curious.

Think BIG

If you are reading this text or listening to this A.C.T.I.O.N. Plan series, you are curious about the possibility of experiencing change in your life. Regardless of whether you think you need to change, it is a fact that the world is changing around you. You can either let the world move past you, or you can take the challenge to evolve to a greater plateau.

It is time to poke your head out from the trenches of your routine and look at the big world. I believe in higher education, but sometimes the best teachers are right in our own backyards … literally! Take an hour and visit a playground; however, I suggest you go with children you know to avoid looking like you have questionable motives. Observe how children interact. They focus on life in the moment. They don't worry about what they look like when they roll down a hill, or think that a caterpillar feels "icky" to hold, or that their runners will get wet if they run through the fountain. They openly ask questions like, "Where did you get that fire truck?" In response—without hesitation—the reply might be, "I got it from Santa." The response may not be the most credible, but the process is valuable. If they want to know something, they simply ask. If they see an opportunity, they go for it.

In adulthood, we become aware of consequences and, in my opinion, we trade curiosity for caution. Both are valuable, but both need to be balanced to be successful. Anyone who is a leader or successful in an endeavour had to look fear directly in the face, invite it in, and strip its power using rational facts. Fear is an emotion, not a strategy, but its presence can motivate the development of a strategy that will overcome its shackles.

Thinking in terms of possibilities and creating a path for your ultimate summit require stamina. You wouldn't start a long road trip without checking the gas and fluid levels in your car or the air pressure in the tires. It is critical that you check under your own hood to make sure you are ready for the journey to move your business forward.

Do not underestimate the power of health. The road to success is long and challenging. If you plan to be a business warrior, do everything in your power to make sure that you have the stamina to win.

Climb Your Mountain

Plan to be a business leader with longevity:
- ✓ Book a physical.
- ✓ See a dentist.
- ✓ Increase your activity.
- ✓ Choose a variety of foods with more "whole" and less "processed" ingredients.
- ✓ Drink more water.
- ✓ Get quality sleep.

The following personal and business inventory lists will assist you in gathering facts to build a foundation of confidence. Solid businesses are built on a solid foundation, and it is critical that you take your health seriously if you plan to be in it for the long haul. If you don't take care of yourself, who is going to take care of your business?

Personal Inventory List

What motivates you?
What skills and strengths do you possess?
What are you not good at?
What do you like to do? (Note that this can be very different from what you are good at.)
What do you avoid (e.g., conflict, change, or routine activities)?
How do you spend your time?
What do others say about you (e.g., I am dependable, creative, on time, full of ideas)? Ask them if you don't know.
What tools do you use to stay organized?
Do you tend to finish what you start?
How do you stay updated (e.g., Internet, social events, or media)?

Business Inventory List

What is your big-picture business goal?
Is the idea, product, or service needed now? What signs indicate this?
Will it be relevant in five or 10 years?
Who is your target client?
What strengths do you bring that will impact this venture's success?
What relevant accomplishments and experiences will help you in this venture?
What are your current limitations?
What makes you/your company/product or service different?
Who do you know that can assist you with this venture?
What are your timelines associated with this venture?

Your Future Business

The following process would be helpful for a new business venture or a new division in an existing business:

Describe your business or idea. (Remember to think BIG.)

- What type of business is it?_____

  _____

  _____

- How large could this business become? (Remember: If you don't think BIG, you will fall short of your goal.) Go ahead. Dare to dream!_____

  _____

  _____

- What products or services does/will your business offer? _____

  _____

  _____

Who is your target market?

- Who is your primary market? Think of the demographics your business is focused on (e.g., age, gender, income level, and interests).

  Your primary target market: _____

  _____

  _____

Consider a secondary market that may not be directly linked but would have a common goal. For instance, your business might be to open a doggie spa. Your primary target market might be pet owners; your secondary market might be makers of pet products, such as doggie cookies and designer apparel. This secondary market shares a common market yet doesn't compete with you.

Who are your secondary markets? _____

_____

_____

- Where will you find your target market, and how will they find you?

_____

_____

- Who else is offering this service? _____

_____

_____

- What makes you stand out among the competition? _____

_____

_____

- How do you know your business is needed?_____

_____

_____

- What signs support the belief that your business will be needed in five years? _____

_____

_____

- Who do you need to support your idea?_____

_____

_____

- How much will your business idea cost? (Estimate.) _____

_____

_____

- What will your role be in this business? _____

_____

_____

Climb Your Mountain

✓ Build a constant and varied knowledge base.
✓ When observing any event, challenge yourself with these questions: How will this affect my business? What do I currently know about this? Whom do I need to talk to?
✓ Source out industry reports, radio, television, webinars, and blogs. Find trustworthy sources that will give you a broad perspective regarding what is going on out there.
✓ Join networking groups that will expand your current target markets, such as chambers of commerce and business networking groups.
✓ Volunteer. It is important to give back to your community, and it gives you a perspective of business voids that need to be filled.
✓ Volunteer at events that can provide your business idea with valuable exposure.
✓ Attend seminars that will provide you with important information as well as possible connections. Listening to experts in your field is vital to the success of your business.
✓ Connect with organizations that share a common focus.

These questions will be discussed in greater detail in the following stages of the A.C.T.I.O.N. Plan, but you need to be thinking about them now so that you are fully prepared for the journey ahead of you.

Know the World Around You

Not only does the Awareness phase require you to think BIG and critically analyze what you bring to the business, it also requires you to observe the signs around you. You and your business are not an island. As your business will influence the world, expect the world to influence your business.

A.C.T.I.O.N. PLAN

Signs are always present; whether or not you choose to recognize them is up to you and, regardless of your choice, they will impact you. That said, isn't it more logical to choose to be proactively aware rather than being reactive because you weren't prepared for the changes you are facing? Train yourself to look for these signs in your industry, your neighborhood, your city, your country, and globally. Don't go through your day with blinders on. Question what you are observing.

- Is there obvious growth in your city? How will this prosperity impact your business venture?
- Has a major employer laid off staff in your industry? What implications could this have on your plans?
- Has a major contract been awarded that could bring people to your city? What could that mean for your current and future strategies?

In Summary

- Think BIG without limitations.
- Clearly understand your business potential, and truthfully evaluate what skills you bring to it and what you are missing.
- Get a picture of everything around you and ask, "How will this affect my business?"

The more you become aware, the better prepared you are for success.

Know your strengths, but manage them so
they don't become your weaknesses.

A.C.T.I.O.N. PLAN

Awareness Business Strategy

https://goo.gl/ser86Q
(time 12:22)

Awareness Interview with Rob Petkau

https://goo.gl/GDWdQC
(time 22:28)

Using a scan app, scan the QR code above, or use the above link to access the sound file.

Note: Please allow a few moments for the file to open on your device.

A.C.T.I.O.N. PLAN

CHAPTER 2

Commitment

Above the clouds at Kilimanjaro's Kibo base camp, the supermoon lights the night sky over Mawenzi peak. The six-hour, midnight climb to Uhuru's summit (5,895 meters/19,341 feet) is only hours away. Present altitude is 4,700 meters (15,420 feet), and the temperature is below freezing. Temperature estimated for a sunrise summit is -21 degrees C plus wind.

Lessons from the Mountain ...

The Mount Kilimanjaro experience was becoming less of a concept and more of a reality. After some investigation, we connected with a tour company that had originated in Africa and expanded to the United States and Canada. Baraka Maro of Good Earth Tours filled in many of our question blanks and offered a perfect combination of experience. He was a seasoned travel agent who grew up in Arusha, the main centre closest to the base of Kilimanjaro. As an added bonus, he was proficient in the climb. This experience, and the fact that Baraka now lived in North America, created the perfect transitional reference for us. His knowledge of the two cultures was valuable to prepare for our impending experience.

With Baraka's assistance, we checked off the questions that had been mounting during our original awareness phase. As we gained more knowledge, we soon realized that we had more questions. In retrospect, the awareness phase never left us; it had created a growing and valuable source of pertinent information that guided us through the journey.

Our original travel team of two had doubled, as my daughter Jessica and Cameron, a friend of Kathy's, had decided to join in the quest for summiting Uhuru Peak, the highest point on Kilimanjaro. My husband Larry had decided not to join us on this trek but was completely supportive and never wavered in his belief that we would be successful. It was great to have that voice of reason, as my Internet searches had occasionally left me feeling a tinge of apprehension about the trek. This seemed to be more noticeable the closer we got to our travel date.

Reading excerpts from blogs had occasionally allowed doubt to penetrate my optimism. For example, "Uhuru was not mine to be had that day. Sick and far from home I was helped down the mountain by our guides" ... "Tragedy hits Kilimanjaro as member of Italian team dies in fall" ... "We saw climbers being rushed down the mountain on stretchers, foaming at the mouth as fluids filled their lungs due to the altitude" … "Porter on climb dies of heart attack."

These accounts challenged my commitment for this venture. This was a far stretch from anything I had ever done although I had always been active. In my younger years, I played on several high school sports teams; in my adult life, running, hiking, and cycling had been favourite pastimes. To help our minds and bodies prepare for the climb, Jessica and I had been pushing our stamina at the gym and doing outdoor stair climbing by the Edmonton River Valley. We had hiked up Ha Ling Peak in the Rocky Mountains, but its elevation of 2,407 meters (7,897 feet) was a far cry from Uhuru's 5,895 meters (19,341 feet), which was considered well within the extreme altitude levels where oxygen was only about half of what we were used to.

Checking in with Baraka had become a regular occurrence, and his patience was appreciated. He reminded me that we had selected the Marangu route with an extra day of acclimatization because it had the greatest success for their tours. There had been many routes to choose from. Some sounded positively beautiful; others had offered more aggressive terrain, requiring more hiking days to complete. When we considered all of the options, the Marangu route was chosen as the best for our group. We had paid for our flights and the tour. Our commitment was anchored by our monetary investment in the excursion. But, as the departure date came into our grasp, I found myself balancing the weight of doubt with the desire for success.

A few weeks before we were scheduled to leave, Jessica and I went to get our travel inoculations. It would be the final check for our preparation. Upon our arrival, we were informed that we would have a preliminary interview with the nurse practitioner—a standard meeting to ensure that we received the necessary inoculations for the various countries we were traveling through, namely Kenya and Tanzania.

Sitting across the desk from the nurse, we handed her our itinerary. Watching her expression as she flipped through the pages was like watching an overdramatization of a silent film. Eyes opened wide, staring in disbelief, eyebrows arched and then quickly furrowed, then arched again. Her head slowly shook from side to side.

Without looking up, she murmured, "Oh, no! No, no, no!"

Jessica and I glanced nervously at each other.

"What the heck is this all about?" I wondered.

The nurse turned her attention quickly to the computer monitor, which was not visible to us, and rapidly tapped the keys. In silence, her focus remained fixed on her screen. Watching in anticipation, her expressions showed visible concern, which didn't help our confidence.

She pushed her screen to the side, looked at me, and said, "You have chosen the most deadly route up Kilimanjaro."

Her words punctured our thinly veiled optimism.

"What do you mean?" I asked defiantly, as my mind reeled through the process we used to select this route. "The Marangu route was recommended by our travel guide. He said it was safe."

"Well, it's not," she emphatically argued. "I have just checked, and this is a reputable site."

"What is the problem with this route?" I asked, trying to make sense out of this new and alarming comment.

"There is a low percentage of success and a high rate of deaths," she explained, "and this is not just you going up. You're taking your daughter too."

Her words left me numb. Had I made a terrible mistake? Was I putting Jessica and myself in a dangerous situation? Why would Baraka not have told us this?

"Do you realize that we have added an additional day of acclimatization halfway up the mountain?" I asked, trying to make sense of this chaotic moment.

The nurse picked up the itinerary again, slowly counted the days with her index finger, and then reverted back to her computer. After a moment of checking with her screen, she stated frankly, "Oh, well then. You might be okay." Quickly looking at Jessica, she added, "But watch your mother

A.**C**.T.I.O.N. PLAN

carefully—particularly when she sleeps. People have been known to stop breathing at high altitudes."

My first instinct was to get up and leave the appointment, but I had to consider the time crunch regarding our departure date. Instead, I looked at her steadily and told her that we were there to get the inoculations as expediently as possible.

We got the shots, stayed 15 minutes to check for any adverse reactions, and walked silently to our car.

"What was that?" Jessica asked in disbelief.

"Bad advice from what should have been a trusted source."

It rattled me enough that I had to make one final call to Baraka. He assured me that they had a very high success rate, but there was always a chance that something could happen. He reminded me of the trained guides that would be helping us. They were experienced and would be looking for any signs to make sure we were safe. At the end of the call, I had reconfirmed my belief that we had made all the correct decisions so far.

Fear would not get in the way of this experience. I was going to commit to it completely. The truth of the matter is that there will always be situations that might make you second guess an idea, and there will be people who offer poorly conceived advice. Questioning is an important part of the process to weed through the plethora of information and discern quality facts from emotional opinions.

This commitment phase of our trip was important to test us for what was to come. There were two camps of individuals that offered advice on our trip. Most were excited to hear about the adventure, but occasionally we would come across someone not as enthused and less convinced that we would be successful. Honestly, they were just as valuable as the energized cheerleaders because they reminded us of the reality we were to face. If the comments were fact based, then I considered them seriously. For instance, the concern about safe drinking water led to the decision to bring purification tablets with us.

A.**C**.T.I.O.N. PLAN

The negative comments didn't detract us from our goal; in fact, they helped to strengthen our commitment and be better prepared for what was to come.

I believed that if other people had been successful climbing Kilimanjaro, we would be too. It was now time to move on, closer to the goal. Learn, pivot, and adjust as we go. There was no turning back; no fear to drag me off course. I would trust my guides and my instinct. I would continue to increase my awareness and strengthen my commitment. Kilimanjaro never promised to be an easy experience, but it sure was going to be fantastic to stand at the top of that mountain!

> *" An idea without committed action remains only an idea. An idea + committed action builds traction. "*

How to Create Commitment in Your Business

Consider this question: "If time, money, or resources were no obstacle, what would you do?" This question was alluded to in the Awareness phase, asking you to think without limitations to get a clear sense of possibilities and remove yourself from thinking in the "ruts." The difference between the dreamers and the doers is what happens next. Now it is time to test the waters and investigate how interested you are in venturing forward to a new plateau.

The second phase in the A.C.T.I.O.N. Plan is Commitment. This is the place where all the good ideas and possibilities that have been collected in the Awareness phase become grounded into a strategy that initiates traction. Without the Commitment phase, the Awareness phase will be like a kite rising with possibilities but without direction or purpose. The Commitment phase is critical to ensure that your business has direction and purpose and is not simply a cluster of ideas.

A common reason for business failures arises from a poorly developed commitment level. Businesses need to develop a reliable structure before any "seed" of an idea can take root and flourish. The adage, "Measure twice, cut once," is a strong reminder of how important the planning stage is to obtain successful results. Regardless of where you are in your business cycle—starting up or well established—this phase grounds your future development.

When you first start a business venture, your commitment level and clarity will set the tone to build your business model. This phase helps ensure that you don't miss any important steps. It is easy to get swept up in the excitement of a new idea, but this is when you must begin to plan for your success and not passively "hope" it will happen.

As an established business owner, you have no doubt realized that your personal commitment and clarity have a rippling effect on others. The "C" for Commitment could equally represent the word "Confidence." Confidence develops when your personal commitment level gains traction. Conversely, established business owners who struggle with committed team members or clients will find that they moved through this phase too quickly and didn't develop their personal vision clearly enough—or did not know how to transfer their vision to others.

Entrepreneurs often struggle with the Commitment stage but not necessarily because they cannot be committed; on the contrary, they are so personally engaged in their vision that they miss the fact that others need a door or window to catch a glimpse of their vision. Excitement is not a sure bet for contagious commitment. You need to be aware of how those around you are responding to your ideas. Be prepared to sell your ideas. Don't be discouraged if your supporters do not show up in droves. Your ideas need to be presented in a manner that inspires your audience to want to learn more.

When you have a great idea, you want to share it. If your commitment is well rooted, you will speak and act with growing confidence, attracting like-minded thinkers. This communication will soon ripple to your team, grounding them with a focused goal.

The Commitment phase is a phase of change, and change requires action. You may feel that the venture upon which you are about to embark will require a great deal of planning; others may simply want to take what they are currently doing to a more lucrative and impactful level. If you do not review and revise what you are currently doing, you will not make the traction to move ahead. Doing more of the same can keep you idling or even create a deep rut.

Established business owners know that, as a business develops, things have to adjust—particularly if you are going to keep up. Technology alone motivates the need for revision, regardless of whether or not change was in the plans. Established businesses facing expansion, technological advancements, standardization, global implications, and increased customer demands need to move through the phases of the A.C.T.I.O.N. Plan just as a novice business owner does.

The established owner's Awareness lists will likely be rich with skills and abilities on which to build, but running a $2 million to $5 million business is not the same as running a $50 million to $100 million business. The following phases (Team, Implementation, Opportunities, and Next) will help the developing owner and key associates look at the impending horizon as a new business opportunity, which isn't as easy as just adding water to make more soup. There is a double-edged sword for established businesses. On one side, you have a business that is growing and showing signs of opportunities; on the other side, this business is already keeping you and your team busy while maintaining its existence, and you will need a clear plan to move forward without dropping balls. How do you see your

An idea, regardless of how great it may seem, will only remain an idea if it does not meet a committed action.

new operation in five to 10 years? Your vision can only transpire into reality with a plan of action.

This Commitment phase does not have to result in drastic changes to your current situation. In fact, the rationale behind the A.C.T.I.O.N. Plan is to act in a methodical and progressive manner, which creates traction that is developed from initiating a well-thought-out plan. This plan does not suggest that you abandon your current situation and act in haste; on the contrary, the process relies on the traction created by integrating the processes of evaluation, strategy development, implementation, and evaluation—all critical phases of change management.

Whether you use sports or military metaphors, best strategies engage awareness of your situation at all times so that you don't get blindsided. Although we have now moved into the Commitment phase, we never leave Awareness.

Climb Your Mountain

✓ Consider your response to the question, "If time, money, or resources were no obstacle, what would you do?"_____

✓ Place yourself in the realm of possibilities. This can happen.

✓ Be open to "how" this can happen._____

✓ Review your inventory lists from the Awareness phase, and look for direct correlations between your skills and abilities and this possible venture. If you were honest, you will know the areas in which you are going to need help._____

✓ List the missing skills that you will need to move your vision forward.

_____

✓ List the people required to fulfill these needs. The following section will deal with strategies to build your team, but making a list of whom you have and whom you will need in the future is important.

_____

✓ Who do you have fulfilling positions such as bookkeeping and accounting, research and development, sales, social media, information technology, marketing and advertising, customer relations, human relations, and legal advice?_____

✓ Who provides your financial advice? _____

When a business starts out, there is a risk associated with taking on family members and friends to fill roles. This may be acceptable in a temporary situation to help you gain some traction, but be aware that these roles are critical to your success. This can be seen even with established businesses. Over time, the wrong people have stayed in the wrong positions. Owners know that this is an obstacle, but they struggle with how to deal with the situation. However, family members may be perfectly suited for a role. The decision to place an individual into any position of responsibility should always be based on competency and not convenience.

A.**C**.T.I.O.N. PLAN

Define Your Business

Know Who You Are and What Your Business Offers

If you are going to be successful at business, you need to be crystal clear about:

- Who you are;
- What your business is; and
- Who your business is for.

The #1 reason businesses struggle to gain traction is that they try to be too many things to too many people.

It is not a good business practice to accept all clients. Listen to your instincts. Sometimes it is more lucrative to say "no" than to say "yes." New businesses are particularly vulnerable to this trap for fear of losing potential dollars. When every dollar counts, it is hard to see that saying "no" now can save you money in the future.

Focus Your Business by Creating a Mission Statement

A mission statement is an important component to your business's identity. Not only does it define your business for the outside world, it becomes a guide for your team to follow. Your mission statement declares why your business exists.

Points to consider when developing a mission statement:

- State who you are, what you do, how you do it, and who will benefit.
- Keep it personal to your business and memorable.

Template guide: "We are **(business name)**. We provide **(description of your business)** to **(description of your client)** by **(describe how you do it)**."

Example: "We are **Out-of-this-World Tours**. We provide **virtual vacations** to **individuals and groups wishing to experience an unknown locale prior to committing to a destination** by **utilizing the latest virtual tour programs available**."

Your mission statement: "**We are Out-of-this-World Tours, leaders in providing realistic virtual tours to clients, by bringing the world to you**."

If you want to gain traction, your tread has to be specific.

Define Your Client

You need to be clear about who your client is and who it is not. This will be used in the Implementation phase, so the more detailed you can be about who your ideal client is, the more precise the strategies will be to achieve your goals.

To assist you in defining your client, complete the following table:

Who needs this product or service?
Who would buy this product or service?
Who would influence the purchase of this product or service?
Will my product or service require online reach?
Where will I find these clients?
How will they find me?
What other interests would this target market have (e.g., potential cross-market opportunities)?
What would this target market's hot buttons be (i.e., what do they like and dislike)?
Who else would they go to for a similar service?
Who are their referral networks?
What organizations do they support?
Who can connect me with these people?

An example of the type of client that would be interested in our virtual tour business example might be as follows:

OUR CLIENTS

Our clients are individuals wishing to experience various locales prior to committing to a destination, such as:

- Business meetings and incentive trip planning
- Family and individual vacation planning
- Destination wedding planning

Create Your Promise to Your Client

When you know what your business is and who your client is, the next logical step is to verbalize your business promise to validate your mission statement. If the mission statement is the "what" and the client target is the "who," then consider the business promise the "how."

OUR PROMISE TO OUR CLIENTS

We provide:

- The latest technology for a realistic experience
- The most comprehensive library of world destinations, including popular and remote selections
- Expert planners for all destinations

When you are clear about what your business is, who your client is, and what your clients can expect, your commitment will be evident. You will speak with clarity about your business, which will attract supporters, clients, and potential team members and investors.

Create Your Business Plan

Do You Need One?

Did you know that one of the top reasons new and existing businesses fail is because the owners didn't create a business plan? Business plans have been given a bad reputation. Developing one may not be viewed as the most exhilarating activity to experience, but it should never be considered unnecessary. I challenge you to see it as both a streamlined ocean cruiser, sailing effortlessly through uncharted waters, as well as a lifeboat, helping you to steer clear of impending dangers. How can that be considered dull? A business plan offers a structured opportunity, like a trusted map that keeps you focused on your destination.

Top Reasons for Having a Business Plan

- **A business plan is one of the best litmus tests to see if your idea can grow into a viable business.** This process allows you to discover flaws in your idea while the process is in the planning stage. It also provides time to develop a strategy to rectify any concerns. Businesses that don't give themselves the opportunity to investigate challenges in the safety of this planning stage will likely experience them once they have committed to the business; however, at that point, precious time, money, and emotions will be spent backtracking or focusing on putting out fires rather than focusing on maintaining and gaining business momentum.
- **A business plan provides you with a clear idea of what your business is so that you can remain focused and make appropriate, critical decisions.** It allows you to gather critical data that will provide a vital portrayal of where you are now and what you can project for the future. A detailed plan will protect you and your

business from veering off track. These steps are valuable when businesses expand and diversify over time.

- **A business plan offers you the chance to think about your marketing strategy.** Marketing is more than advertising—much more. It involves branding and business development and requires a statistical analysis of trends and expectations. A business plan helps you prepare your business to proactively manage the demands imposed by the ebbs and tides of the market. This will be discussed further in the Implementation phase as well.

- **A business plan is a necessity in the event you require financial support.** Regardless of whether you plan to request funding from a financial institution, approach investors, apply for a business grant, or go into a partnership, you need a business plan to prove that your business has the potential to be viable. *The best time to secure financial support is when you don't need it.* Financial institutions are faced with tough decisions daily regarding who will get loans and who will not. Make it easy for them to put your request into the acceptance pile. For an explanation of the creation of a business plan, see "Step-by-Step Business Plan" on page 191.

Note that it is critical to obtain advice from professionals when developing your business. Before you have made a claim or developed or signed any agreements, solicit appropriate legal, financial, and accounting advice. Professional advice is critical to the success of a business. Remember: Regardless of how great an idea may seem, it will only remain an idea if it does not meet a committed action. Your business plan is that committed action!

I know this seems ludicrous, as businesses typically ask for financial support when they need it, but institutions and individuals will be more likely to get involved when risk is minimized. Capital is required to start a business venture, and lending institutions as well as private investors will be looking to see what your business is worth, what you have personally

The best time to get approved for financial support is when you don't need it.

invested, and whether your business is viable to prosper and pay your financial obligations. You will be more successful to secure loans if you provide proof that your business has a solid future—and that starts with a business plan.

In Summary

Do not underestimate the importance of this Commitment phase. If you are ready to make a change in your future, you need to be prepared for it. Remember: "Measure twice, cut once."

You can jump into the water with the knowledge that you can swim; however, if you haven't checked for rocks under the waves, or the presence of a strong undercurrent, or changing weather patterns, or the presence of sharks (you get the picture), you are gambling with a successful outcome. Business isn't just a "one leap" endeavour (if you got through that one, you're good). You will be faced with many leaps and dives over the course, and a business plan will guide you through uncharted waters and rugged terrain in your business's future. The effort will be well worth it.

" *Commitment separates the dreamers from the doers.* "

Commitment Business Strategy

https://goo.gl/3DjUDz

(time 24:10)

Commitment Interview with Dr. Nixon

https://goo.gl/ytf4du

(time 23:10)

Using a scan app, scan the QR code above, or use the above link to access the sound file.

Note: Please allow a few moments for the file to open on your device.

A.C.T.I.O.N. PLAN

CHAPTER 3

Team

Our group of four trekked the Marangu route of Mount Kilimanjaro with 16 support members, including a lead and an assistant guide, porters, and cooks. The team back home consisted of our supportive family, friends, and our travel agent Baraka of Good Earth Tours.

" Great ideas come from individuals.
Great accomplishments come from great teams! "

Lessons from the Mountain ...

From the moment Kathy and I agreed to tackle Kilimanjaro, we had the beginning of a partnership. This was then extended to my daughter Jessica and Kathy's friend Cameron. The four of us would become a core unit that we would conversely support and rely on. Choosing our team was not a random act. Kathy and I were committed to the adventure, so sharing our goal to entice and engage others was not difficult. We also knew that both Jessica and Cameron would be great additions to the team. We knew that it would be critical to have team members who embrace a common goal. Each member would either add to the success or the failure of the journey. Selecting our travel companions was a serious consideration, but we knew we could not do this trek on our own. It became abundantly clear at the onset that we would be wise to engage in others' expertise to maximize our experience and ensure the greatest opportunities for a successful summit.

Baraka of Good Earth Tours represented such expertise. Whenever you take on an important venture, you want to surround yourself with a support/ advisory system that will guide and keep you focused on your target. It is critical to know what you bring to the table but equally what you need from others. Assuming that you can do it all yourself will only derail your efforts. Baraka provided an experienced team to assist us on our quest led by Dismas Urio.

Meeting Dismas for the first time was inspiring. His gentle and calm spirit was a sharp contrast to what I had expected of a man who had summited Kilimanjaro several times. He had no ego, just a sincere and practical approach to ensure that his charge of four Canadians would make it successfully to Uhuru Peak unscathed.

If Baraka directed the vision for this trip, along with our input, Dismas was our lead guide and therefore our strategist. He would set the pace, evaluate our abilities, and establish the best path to take—an enormous responsibility, particularly on the last part of our climb. Meeting him the day before we would begin our climb was the beginning of a trusting relationship. While we basked in the August sun, which was pouring into the courtyard of our Arusha lodge, Dismas methodically divulged the plan for the next six days.

He described the importance of following his directions. We would have an assistant guide on the trip (Joe), but we should not think of Joe as a junior as he had many successful summits under his belt. Dismas warned us that it may seem excruciatingly slow at times but that we must maintain the pace "pole-pole" (po-lay, po-lay, which is Swahili for "slowly"). He reminded us of the altitude we would be climbing (5,895 meters, or 19,341 feet). To put it in perspective, Mount Robson has the highest peak in the Canadian Rocky Mountains, rising to 3,954 meters (12,972 feet), and Mount Rainier in Washington's Cascade Range rises to 4,394 meters (14,417 feet).

Dismas also explained that we would be traveling with our own entourage. Other than himself and Joe, there would be porters to help us carry all of our gear and cooks to prepare the meals in advance of our arrival at each camp. We were told that our personal packs should only hold those items we would need each day; the larger packs that held our sleeping gear would be carried up with the porters. We politely argued that we could carry our own things. With a stern expression, Dismas reminded us that we needed to trust his lead.

The next morning, the four of us filled in the last four seats of a packed van, which was waiting outside our lodge entrance.

"So this is our team," we thought.

Dismas pointed to the second vehicle. In total, we had a lead guide, an assistant guide, a cook, his assistant, and 12 porters. When we arrived at the gates of Tanzania's Kilimanjaro National Park and disembarked the van, it was clearer to us why that number of people was needed. Each person knew exactly what they were to do, and they executed their actions with precision.

While Dismas took care of the administrative duties of registering each member of our crew with the park authorities, Joe stayed with us, sharing humorous and engaging stories about his previous climbs. This was not just idle conversation to fill the time; it was an important step in knowing more about our team as Joe was establishing the foundations of a trusting relationship.

While Joe answered our questions and shared stories about previous treks, the porters and cook took our gear, their gear, and the six-day supply of food to the weigh stations. The motto of Kilimanjaro is, "Do not leave anything on and do not take anything from our mountain." The original recorded weight would be compared to the bags' weight when we returned, taking into consideration the weight difference of the food we consumed.

It was clear that we all had our roles for the climb. Dismas and Joe would be primary strategists, while the crew implemented the important daily tasks that kept the process running smoothly. The four of us offered important feedback to Dismas, which was used to fine-tune strategies. Like the cogs of a well-oiled machine, our team moved in unison.

Along with our travelling crew, we would be remiss to not acknowledge our home team. All of our family and friends who had supported our efforts to get us to the gates of this majestic mountain would never be forgotten.

Now, the next part of our journey would be in the hands of our Good Earth team.

A.C.**T**.I.O.N. PLAN

" An individual may have come up with
the thought of sending a man to the moon,
but it took a team to make it a reality. "

How to Create Team in Your Business

Come on. Admit it. You've thought, "Let me do that. I can do it better!" If you have a shred of entrepreneurial fibre in your business makeup or leadership potential, it has entered your mind. We have all thought it. It's good to appreciate your skills and talents, but if you let this thought persist, it will breed arrogance, not confidence.

One of the biggest challenges new business owners face is recognizing that they can't do it all by themselves. This is unfortunately a major reason why businesses fail within the first three years. Without meaning to sabotage their own dreams, new owners fail to recognize that *they* have become the bottleneck in their "one-person show," so to speak. This can be a horrific flaw for established business owners as well. It's actually a simple physics lesson. Even the most talented juggler will drop balls when they take on more than they can handle. Gravity is a powerful force; it often defeats the momentum of good intentions. What goes up must come down. An owner who takes on more than they should will inevitably start to drop balls.

The "Team" phase of the A.C.T.I.O.N. Plan is the place where you come to terms with the fact that you need help to be successful. Entrepreneurs are notorious for thinking, "I can do this better than anyone else." This thought can plague businesses for years, resulting in a revolving door of team members who never get the opportunity to expand their skills to drive momentum in the business. Instead, the business limps along as the owner continues to work "in" the business rather than "on" the business. These businesses lament that they can't find good workers. Perhaps the business owner is attempting to juggle too many balls. Growth of a team takes time.

If you recall your Awareness exercises, you will remember that you are not great at everything and there are things that you prefer to do. When people engage in activities that they are not particularly good at, many things happen:

The first rule of business success is to fire yourself!

- Their passion becomes stagnant, and belief in their dream starts to evaporate.
- Errors happen more regularly because the wrong person is doing the task.
- Backlogs begin to happen because the wrong person cannot be efficient or effective. Backlogs cost the company dearly in the form of money, clients, and eventually reputation.
- A person stuck in the wrong job doesn't have time to do what they love and what they do best.
- When a person consistently takes on more than they are capable of handling, their health begins to deteriorate.

To build a strong business, you must ask yourself, "What am I great at?" and "What am I not great at?" You need a team to support what you are great at, which means placing people in critical positions to fill in those areas that you are not truly great at. Surrounding yourself with the best can be a precarious balancing act.

When it comes to building a solid team for success, the following pillars must be present: visionaries, strategists, implementers, and evaluators.

Visionaries

Visionaries gather facts and experiences to imagine a new future and exhibit the following characteristics:

✓ Take a leader role
✓ Are BIG thinkers
✓ See beyond the current situation
✓ Are creative and imaginative
✓ Think in terms of "what could be"
✓ Suggest progressive ideas
✓ Can verbalize vision to others, creating interest to support goals
✓ Exude confidence

This is typically easy for entrepreneurs to fill, as they are the ones who often come up with innovative ideas. They colour outside of the lines because they believe that doing things the same way, all the time, is devastating for the growth of a business, especially in a changing world.

Visionaries observe what is missing and suggest solutions. These are great idea people. They see what is possible—not just for tomorrow but well into the future. Visionaries are critical for business as they are the ones who help companies become industry leaders. They instinctively and confidently set goals.

Although these are all admirable qualities, a business won't get far with only great ideas and no plan to achieve the goals. At first glance, everyone might think they have the skills to be in a visionary role; however, by itself, this role lacks the practical skills to finish the job.

Characteristics required of a visionary role are as follows:

- You naturally look at and analyze your environment (e.g., business, industry, city, and world), interpreting the cryptic signs around that help you know where to lead.
- You develop knowledge from gained experience in order to enhance your intuition.
- People naturally come to you for advice and direction.
- You possess a curious nature to ask "Why?" and "Why not?"
- You have the ability to balance your curious nature with a practical reality that will guide the preparation and timing of action.
- You act decisively on facts.
- You can juggle many tasks simultaneously and have the ability to determine critical timing and employ teamwork to ensure completion.
- You may possess strategy skills that will guide action toward the vision.

Examples of visionaries include:

- Positions of leadership, particularly in uncharted areas
- Any position responsible for innovation
- Any position responsible for improving current standards
- Any position that accepts the challenge to create new from old and exceptional from mediocre
- Any position that is responsible for diversification

Strategists

Strategists understand the lay of the land and the ultimate goal, and create a map to guide past obstacles while building momentum from opportunities. They exhibit the following characteristics:

- ✓ Think in terms of solutions
- ✓ Are involved in developing the goals (i.e., give structure to the vision)
- ✓ Are able to formulate a plan of action
- ✓ Embrace thinking BIG to formulate strategies
- ✓ Can sift through a situation and identify what is critical and what is not
- ✓ Understand the vision and engage the team into acting toward the common goal
- ✓ Can adapt to change easily and often instigate change as a strategy, which is known as a change agent
- ✓ May possess visionary abilities

A strategist works with great ideas and develops a plan to achieve the goals. Strategists take the big picture, breaking it down into manageable pieces to create a plan. They come with a wealth of diverse connections collected over the years and know where to get information or resources to prepare the best strategies. Strategists work closely with visionaries, and the two complement each other's skills.

Examples of strategists include:

- Business consultants
- Executive level of organization, which often possesses these skills even if the roles do not call for it
- Senior management
- Leaders in an implementer or evaluator role (middle management-level positions that often require individuals to develop strategies for their own departments to follow)

- Individuals who can take an idea, regardless of its present tangibility, and create a path for its future regardless of the title the individual holds

Implementers

Efficiency is the implementer's motto, and effectiveness is their result. High-functioning implementers are critical to a successful team. Regardless of their position, implementers understand the importance of performing their role with consistency. They recognize that their actions ultimately reflect the business's brand and corporate image. They understand that they provide a solid foundation for the business and therefore astutely provide valuable insight that can improve systems and procedures.

Effective implementers exhibit the following characteristics:

✓ Execute the plan with precision
✓ Are detail oriented
✓ Follow direction well but are prepared to make recommendations to improve the efficiency of the plan
✓ Put quality first but understand that quantity is a measure of efficiency
✓ Represent the "how" of a business image
✓ Astutely detect deficiencies and anomalies before they become a concern

Having great ideas and a plan are certainly critical starting points, but unless you have committed implementation at every level of your business, the ideas and strategies will be useless. Implementers represent the true image of your business and provide the verification of your branding efforts.

Examples of implementers include:

- Frontline brand representatives who know how to greet clients on the phone and in person
- Office administration team (including transaction agents)
- Business development specialists (in conjunction with strategy skills)
- Sales teams who approach clients with solutions and follow up with them to maintain a solid relationship
- Warehouse/manufacturing teams who are instrumental in chain-supply management involved in producing and delivering to an established standard
- Customer service staff who ensure that the products and services meet the established standards
- Compliance roles where anomalies are detected and standards are established
- Human resources teams who check that hiring and training standards are met
- Accounting staff who meet set standards for all records and financial processes
- Legal assistance personnel who set and adhere to standards required for running the business ethically and legally
- Information technology teams who keep technology updated and performing to standards
- Marketing staff who make certain that the image of the business is maintained
- Any position that is required to follow a process to achieve the desired outcome consistently

Evaluators

Evaluators provide vital analysis to evaluate the effectiveness of existing strategies and situations. They exhibit the following characteristics:

- ✓ Are highly detail oriented
- ✓ Are analytical
- ✓ Possess interpretive skills
- ✓ Are able to present results in a useful manner (e.g., with charts, tables, and reviews)
- ✓ Focus on the facts
- ✓ Work closely with strategists
- ✓ May possess strategist skills

The evaluator skill is critical to monitor your results in order to know if you are achieving the results you expect. This individual has access to information that is valuable to the visionary and the strategist and can present it in a meaningful manner. Results obtained and presented are critical at various stages of the life cycle of a business. It is imperative that monthly, quarterly, and annual reports are prepared to use as a compass for future plans.

Examples of evaluators include:

- Accounting personnel
- Marketing personnel
- Information technology personnel
- Management of a company that observes patterns or anomalies affecting the bottom line or the intended goal (may represent any department in a business that requires observing and interpreting analytics)
- A position responsible for assessing situations, making necessary corrections or adjustments to move ahead (using a combination of evaluation and strategy skills)

- Subject specialists in an advisory role to assist in vision and strategy development
- Specific implementation roles

A frequently asked question is, "Can't I be all four … or at least three out of four if I have skills in all of the pillars?" The quick answer is, "Not if you want to be successful."

It is possible and very likely to possess skills that represent more than one pillar, and each pillar has the potential for leadership, completely exclusive to the company's ownership title. It is also possible that *at specific times* leaders of an implementation or evaluation pillar may be expected to become strategists; however, their strategies will likely pertain to their specific focus as opposed to the overall strategies that are expected of the strategist pillar.

Entrepreneurs often have the ability to be "big-picture" thinkers. This doesn't mean that an entrepreneur can't be highly focused on specific details about which they are intrinsically passionate. But there are many facets to running a successful business, and it is impossible to keep one eye on the horizon and another on the many details surrounding the business. Big-picture thinkers err when they dismiss the value of "detail specialists," specifically implementers and evaluators.

I have presented the pillars as they fulfill their role in an effective team; however, each of these pillars possesses the real possibility of tipping the team away from the goal—if the other pillars don't balance them.

Consider the impact on your business if your entire team consisted of:

- **Visionaries:** Expect a plethora of amazing ideas that never get going. This group of visionaries would never have anyone grounding them with a direction. Too many ideas at once are like listening to an orchestra tuning their instruments before a performance where everyone is focused on their own instrument, resulting in making amazing sound but not coordinated ensemble music.

- **Strategists**: If they also possess visionary skills, which is extremely likely, strategists would have no problem sitting down and creating a map to get to the goal. If they didn't have a vision, they will be making plans to go nowhere. Too many strategies at one time can cause confusion. Which one should be implemented first? If a business only fulfills the roles of the visionary and strategist, they would be required to fulfill all tasks, even if that is not their skill set. Again, it would be like a conductor leading the symphony and being solely responsible for its ultimate success, including marketing the performance, selling the tickets, ensuring sound quality, and evaluating the financial success of the performance. Visionaries and strategists alone cannot move a company successfully toward a successful goal. The performance will go on, but who is going to market the performance and sell tickets? Who will ensure that the sound is adequate for the back row and still not blast the listeners in the front? Who will be reviewing the performance in terms of its entertainment value? How will anyone know if they met their goal or fell short?

- **Implementers:** When you are excellent at executing a task, it can soon become a dangerous comfort zone. If a strategy is not updated, implementers will continue to do the same task over and over. This is not to suggest that implementers are mindless; on the contrary, they are highly intelligent and critical thinkers and, unless there is a fundamentally good reason to change a procedure, they will continue. Implementers who act in a routine may become disenchanted as they lose their higher purpose. They need to feel as though they are contributing to a common goal and not simply creating a rut of sameness. Imagine how long an orchestra member would stay in the ensemble if they only had one symphony to perform over and over again.

- **Evaluators:** Rarely would you experience too many true evaluators in a business where their skill set overlapped; however, everyone has an opinion. If an evaluator is constantly reviewing projects that show little change, they run the risk of not evaluating but "anticipating" the results. Evaluators who have not had their skills utilized by an efficient team with vision, strategy, and implementation soon find themselves being jaded and saying things like, "We did that before. It doesn't work." Evaluators need to have their skills add value to a project, which requires a team providing them with something worth evaluating. Imagine the excitement that results when the accountant delivers the news to the visionary of the performance that the production "made money"! That news goes back to the strategist and the process continues. Without an effective team, the project will stagnate.

Selecting Your Team

It takes time to select and develop the team that fits best with your vision; however, if you keep the pillars in mind, you will avoid a common trap into which many owners stumble: hiring people they like versus hiring people they need.

If you always hire with the same profile rather than adhering to the vision, you will create a rut that will stop momentum. Different-minded people will bring a rich diversity that is essential to a strong team.

Remember: The first rule of business success is to fire yourself!

The Reference Checklist on page 88 is a guide to help you select your most effective team. Adapt these questions to your own needs. It is easy to get blindsided in an interview. The best way to ensure that you are reading a potential hire effectively is to follow up with the Reference Checklist. This will tell you a great deal about the candidate from those who have experienced working with them in the past. We don't check references nearly enough and, when we do, few people know the best questions to ask. Avoid only "hiring a pulse." Do not settle for someone simply because you are in need. The wrong hire could exacerbate a tough situation into a larger concern. Don't hire based on a casual referral such as, "My bookkeeper's son is looking for work. You should hire him." He may be a perfect fit, but that's up to you to decide. It doesn't have to be awkward. It's not about finding your new best friend; it's about hiring the right person for the right job.

Lead, knowing that your footsteps are worthy of following.

A.C.**T.**I.O.N. PLAN

Reference Checklist

Name of Candidate: _____

Date: _____

Name of Reference: _____

On a scale of 1 to 10 (1 is low and 10 is high), please rate the individual in the following categories. You can go through the questions again and ask what it would have taken to get a higher score (or a 10).

AWARENESS POINTS	SCORE
Ability to accept and manage change in the organization	
Ability to master concepts of the job	
Ability to problem solve within the scope of the job	
Project follow-up skills	
Client relationship skills	
Communication skills	
Goal-setting ability	
Internal team-building skills	
Ability to prioritize	
Punctuality and attendance	
Total Score: _____%	

The final question that must be asked: "Would you hire this person again if given the opportunity?   ❑ Yes   ❑ No

Once you have hired an individual, it is critical to evaluate their progress. Performance reviews have evolved greatly, and there is compelling debate challenging the notion of the effectiveness of annual reviews. Notably the argument points out that waiting a year to assess performance is ineffective. People need constant mentoring, support, and recognition to be effective. Timelines for evaluating progress are dependent on the job and the individual. Whether it is monthly, weekly, or daily, timely interactions and reviews support improved performance and build business culture.

However, this is not a green light to micromanage. Performance reviews are, to a great extent, an evaluation of the business model and process and not only of an employee's performance. Since many small- and medium-sized businesses do not have a human resources specialist to guide the procedure, the reviews become the responsibility of the owner or perhaps the manager who has been delegated with the responsibility. Annual reviews can take on a sense of dread from both parties.

Unfortunately and too often, the employee is informed of their progress so late in the game that they cannot adjust the outcome effectively. These proceedings take on a one-sided approach where the individual conducting the review has all the power, and the employee is never sure what will come next. This is devastating to the culture of a business.

When an employee is hired, they should be aware of their role and responsibilities as well as how they will be held accountable for performance. It is management's place to provide training and mentor to effective responsibility. It is imperative that new hires are enlightened with the company's vision, goals, and strategies. Depending on the role and complexity of tasks, frequent reviews would be suitable. This allows for a relationship to develop between employee and supervisor.

I have found that, when executed in the spirit of support and appreciation, annual reviews provide a summation of activities while establishing future goals. While informal coaching activities should be frequent and relevant, annual reviews provide a summation of growth and the opportunity to collaboratively establish a platform to develop achievable and relevant goals. I recommend that annual reviews be employed to encourage the spirit of support and self-awareness. To that point, I suggest that a review always be prepared by the employee as well as the supervisor. This process encourages dialogue and clarification. If there is any discrepancy between the two reviews, an explanation should result with hopefully an agreed-upon result. This sets the tone of the review as a shared dialogue. I recommend that a blank review be given as part of the employee's onboarding experience so that the new hire knows what is expected. It should be noted that many successful organizations employ 360-degree evaluations. These reviews allow the employees a chance to anonymously evaluate the management and organization.

The Performance Review template on page 91 helps you to focus on your goals by maximizing your team's results. Are the employees delivering results that are moving toward the company's goals? Are team members clear on their tasks? Do they require additional support/training? Do they understand the vision? Are they a good fit for the future? Performance reviews are not intended to focus on faults. *Au contraire!* If, in your review, you identify that the individual is not reaching the intended goal, it is a perfect time to see if the company's needs have changed. Perhaps the company is moving to the next level of growth, and this individual is bogged down. Perhaps it's time to evaluate this position and hire someone to support the goal. Never assume that an unmet goal is purely due to a lack of performance or desire by your team member. Remember: You hired them and, if you hired well, there is a great deal more to the story.

Performance Review

Employee's name: _____

Title: _____

Review date:_____

Type of review: ❑ 90-day   ❑ Progress   ❑ Annual

Supervisor: _____

Rating scale: 1—Performance does not meet expectations
                  2—Inconsistent performance
                  3—Performance meets expectations
                  4—Performance exceeds expectations
                  N/A—not applicable

JOB REQUIREMENTS	REMARKS	RATING
Job knowledge • Demonstrates clear understanding of standards and performs tasks with consistent competency • Demonstrates willingness to learn new techniques to improve results		
Quality of work • Completes projects to meet standards of goals and objectives		
Quantity of work • Volume of work supports goals within specified time frame • Effectively delegates if required • Provides feedback to team members and supervisor to ensure project's completion in a timely manner		

JOB REQUIREMENTS	REMARKS	RATING
Communication with staff and clients • Provides clear verbal communication • Listens accurately • Possesses strong written skills • Uses proper routes of communication		
Teamwork • Accepts direction • Requests assistance appropriately • Willingly cooperates • Willingly participates • Willingly assists others to meet their goals • Is tolerant and respectful to team members • Leads by example		
Reliability • Meets deadlines • Completes tasks as required • Uses discretion at all times • Acts appropriately in situations requiring confidentiality		
Adaptability and flexibility • Supports change • Works well under pressure • Is innovative and creative • Is able to readjust priorities		
Initiative • Demonstrates creativity to improve processes and situations		
Organizational skills • Possesses time management skills • Keeps work area neat and clean • Effectively acts on tasks		

JOB REQUIREMENTS	REMARKS	RATING
Problem solving • Requests assistance appropriately • Uses resources effectively • Makes appropriate decisions based on facts • Acts within scope of position • Makes decisions supported by company • Delivers satisfactory results		

Performance Review Action Summary

Major accomplishments noted during this period:
Job-related strengths:
Areas for improvement/development/training:
Action plan with timelines:
Employees' comments:

Employee signature: _____ Date: _____

Supervisor signature: _____ Date: _____

A true leader instinctively moves in two directions: forward and to the side.

In Summary

As a leader in your business, you need to understand your role now and in the future. If you expect your business to evolve over time, then you must evolve with it. You determine the tone of your business. If you expect to achieve greatness, you will need to surround yourself with greatness, with the understanding that your team will be part of your succession plan.

Team Business Strategy

https://goo.gl/ImQPXW
(time 16:59)

Team Interview with Dale Monaghan

https://goo.gl/bb9mAZ
(time 21:04)

Using a scan app, scan the QR code above, or use the above link to access the sound file.

Note: Please allow a few moments for the file to open on your device.

A.C.T.I.O.N. PLAN

CHAPTER 4

Implementation

Standing on a mountain edge near Zebra Rock. Uhuru Peak,
the summit of Mount Kilimanjaro, looming behind me.

" When faced with an obstacle, acknowledge it, climb it, and take in the new view! "

Lessons from the Mountain ...

The first day of our trek seemed to be a fairly easy hike as we meandered through a comfortable rain-forest zone with temperatures hovering around 22 degrees C (72 degrees F) at the base of the mountain. We followed our lead guide Dismas, while our assistant guide Joe pointed out some of the interesting plant life that was reminiscent of a Jurassic Park backdrop. Massive tree trunks hinted at the mountain's ancient history, supporting a canopy of enormous leaves and thick vines. It was all so stunning, but Dismas ensured that we did not waver from our target and kept the momentum moving forward.

When we arrived at Mandara, our first camp, we were pleased to find that the porters and cooks had arrived much earlier, although how they managed speed with the weighted packs was beyond me. With our gear tucked into our hut, we welcomed the steaming cups of hot cocoa that were waiting for us in the communal dining hall. We had noticed that the air had a decidedly cooler feel when we first saw the buildings peaking through the trees, and reading the information sign located at the camp's entrance offered an explanation. Day 1 on the mountain had started close to noon, and the trek to our first camp had taken just over three hours. With Kilimanjaro being so close to the equator, the daylight hours were approximately the same as the nighttime hours, with sunrise around 6:00 AM and sunset at 6:00 PM. By the time the sun started to hover over the horizon, we had traversed to a height of 2,720 meters (8,924 feet). The higher altitude brought cooler mountain air and, in combination with the high humidity of the rain forest, we experienced the first of many temperature extremes this mountain had to offer. We were humbly grateful for the hot beverages and food our cooks provided as we had worked up ferocious appetites. Holding the steaming cups offered the only external heat our bodies would experience before huddling deep into our sleeping bags that night.

Each day that we advanced up the mountain brought cooler temperatures, and we were aware that constant motion not only positioned us closer to our goal but also ensured our body temperature remained consistent. We would soon learn that timing would be an important concept and the basis for many of the strategies Dismas would employ.

Before we settled in for our first night, we were directed to return to the kitchen to fill up our water packs and bottles with boiled water. Water was collected for cooking and drinking from the various creeks along the trail and could be a dangerous source of harmful bacteria, which could give travellers major health issues. We had heard of many climbers who did not take such precautions, only to be taken down the mountain on stretchers due to intestinal illness. Purification tablets were also included in our boiled water supply as an additional precaution. By the time we were ready to leave the next morning, the water was cool and perfectly safe.

Whether it was the cool mountain air, the brisk activity of hiking for hours, or the fact that it was dark at 6:00 PM, which brought slumber hard and fast, our group of admitted "night owls" was sound asleep by 8:00 PM, only waking to the sound of the porter's 7:00 AM knock, announcing that our wash basins, filled with hot water, were delivered outside our door. After a hearty breakfast, we secured our packs and met our guides at the entrance signposts, ready to take on the next phase of our trip. We were so excited about getting closer to our goal that we hadn't noticed the subtle strategies that Dismas and Joe had been employing to ensure our success.

Our second day held an air of expectation. Dismas had kept the trek at a comfortable pace on the first day; now, on Day 2, he had taken a back seat, letting Joe lead. Joe was a young man who was clearly up for the physical challenge that lay ahead of us.

A.C.T.**I**.O.N. PLAN

Creating the plan to get us up the mountain had fallen completely on Dismas's shoulders. He was a man of few words but evoked a powerful aura of wisdom combined with experience. We had just left Mandara Huts, the first camp of the Marangu route, and we had noticed the visible changes to the terrain and vegetation.

Hanging back to walk with Dismas, I had asked him about the switch in positions. He replied that, as the lead guide, he had to see the climb from all vantage points. As the leader of the team, he needed to observe how we were responding to the changes in elevation. He had noted that Cameron was like a young gazelle with lots of energy, much like Joe.

"Pole-pole," he called out.

Joe looked back, acknowledged the lead's direction, and adjusted his gait.

Dismas explained that it is often the young, athletic men who can get into trouble on the mountain. They don't recognize how thin the air gets, and they don't let their bodies acclimatize. I asked him how true the stories were about deaths on the mountain.

"That's not a discussion for now. People come from all over the world, but not everyone gets to the top."

I could tell that, with Dismas's mindset, he would do everything in his power to ensure our success.

"You have to respect the mountain," he said calmly. "Making it to the top isn't a guarantee. It's not easy. If it were easy, everyone would do it."

I understood that Dismas had positioned himself at the back of the group as a strategy so he could see how we would handle the changes we were about to experience, and he would use that knowledge as we continued our climb.

Kilimanjaro has five distinct ecological zones, which change approximately every 1,000 meters, or 3,280 feet. Each zone offers colder temperatures and less oxygen, something that the body needs time to adapt to, so pole-pole was the strategy of the leader. We were amazed at the strength and agility of the porters. While we kept to our slow pace, they would quickly scurry past us, loaded with pots and bags, many maneuvering the path in worn sandals. I asked Dismas if it was dangerous for the porters to move up the mountain so quickly. He said that our porters live on or close to the mountain and have been acclimatizing their whole life. He acknowledged that, if a porter was not from the area, they needed to have a health check and experience before they could safely take on a trip like this. He confirmed that porter deaths have occurred and can be avoided.

We trekked up the winding path to our next destination, Horombo Camp, and the vegetation changed again. As we scrambled over boulders, we noticed that the trees and shrubs became sparse and larger rocks were common.

By noon, the sun was high and hot. Peeling off the layers of clothing was necessary, as you don't want to sweat and have wet clothes at night. That would provoke a chill that nobody would want. Looking off into the horizon, we could see the snow tip of Uhuru Peak. It seemed so far away. Sighting the peak in the distance was deceiving. It almost seemed as though we still had a long, flat route ahead before we would actually start to climb.

Dismas reminded us that we had been on the mountain since the gates, and we were climbing every step of the way. "The elevation you see from here you will be on in two days."

Horombo Camp greeted us like a mirage, a village in the middle of nowhere. The A-frame huts peaked through the fog that started to settle over the camp. It was late afternoon, and we had been trekking for over five hours. The vegetation zone was Moorland as the camp's elevation was sitting at 3,720 meters (12,205 feet). Like other mountains of high elevation, the climate can change quickly without warning. The mountain seems to make its own weather and, because of that, you never know what is around the next corner. Although we all felt great and believed that we could go farther, we were thankful to land in the camp when we did as the rolling fog made it difficult to see.

After we settled into our huts and had a chance to freshen up (aka relieve ourselves), Joe asked if we wanted to go a little farther and explore the area. We were definitely up for the idea, realizing that this was yet another strategy. By climbing a little farther up the mountain and returning to our camp's lower elevation, we were helping our bodies acclimatize for the higher altitudes we would soon be experiencing. Horombo Camp was our acclimatization point. After exploring for an hour, we returned back to camp—happy, hungry, and tired. The fog had brought night early to the camp and, as a result, sleep was once again easy to obtain.

Day 3 was a great day. It was our acclimatization day. This was the additional day that Baraka had added to our itinerary. To us, it was just a wonderful day to explore, but it was a critical strategy move. The fog had lifted, and we could see that we were in fact above the clouds. It was a stunning view. Amazing, clear, azure skies above us and fluffy, white clouds below made Horombo look like an island surrounded by a frothy ocean.

At first glance, this day may have seemed like an unnecessary addition. After all, we were feeling great. While sipping our cocoa and eating another hearty breakfast of porridge, toast, bacon and grilled meats, and bananas, we listened to Joe's plan for the day. We would be trekking up to Zebra Rock and checking out the views from the rockier terrain. The day almost seemed like a vacation in the middle of the climb.

It was as wonderful as Joe had promised. Some of us faced our fears of climbing onto high perches without support, while others studied the amazing rock formation called Zebra Rock. Joe had explained that the vegetation at this part of the mountain was unique and not found anywhere else in the world. It was a type of arid desert combined with the lush vegetation from the previous zone. He explained that Kilimanjaro was not an ordinary mountain but an enormous stratovolcano. The Zebra Rock formation was in fact a cliff formed by lava. Over time, the mineral-rich rain streaked the black lava rock, leaving a white-striped residue.

This may have been a day surrounded by strategy, but it was so enjoyable and effortless that it could have been tragically avoided and seen as not being necessary. Typically, when a strategy is implemented, there are notable changes. Requirement to adapt to said changes is expected to be noticeable *with the potential of being uncomfortable. This was a critical strategy with massive change, but we didn't notice it. Not only had we allowed our bodies to be better prepared for the days ahead, we literally smelled the roses along the way, increasing our awareness of the immensity of where we were and our appreciation of where we started.*

That night we decided to begin our prescribed Diamox tablets. In our research for this trip, we had learned we would be reaching heights that would compromise our bodies' ability to adapt to the reduced oxygen. We had also learned that, at 3,600 meters (11,811 feet), there were roughly 40% less oxygen molecules available to breathe than what we were used to. At such altitudes, the brain and lungs can leak fluid, causing a dangerous and deadly buildup. There were no guarantees that taking the pills as prescribed would help us because there was just as much positive as negative reported results for the product. In addition, there were studies showing that people successfully summited Kilimanjaro without the tablets. We knew that the best way to deal with altitude was to take the journey slowly, but we were now only one night's sleep away from our Kibo base camp, and we didn't want to take any chances.

Day 4 found our team in a more contemplative place. We knew that, by the end of this day, we would be setting up camp for a relatively short stay. Kibo was our next destination, and it was at the base of the Uhuru Peak. As we walked through the dust bowl known as The Saddle, we gained a better perspective of how massive this mountain was.

Kilimanjaro is so immense that it has more than one peak. It is made up of three volcanic cones with their own peaks: Mawenzi, Shira, and Kibo. Uhuru is Kibo's summit and our ultimate goal. As we traversed the desert saddle, we could see Mawenzi's jagged outline to the east; from our vantage, it appeared to be higher than Uhuru. But vantage points can be deceiving as Mawenzi's peak is 5,149 meters (16,893 feet), which is 746 meters (2,448 feet) less than the Uhuru summit.

A.C.T.**I**.O.N. PLAN

"Pole-pole" were the only words we heard through the wind. The sun was bright, but it offered little warmth. The layers we had once shed in previous days were now only a base to the additional clothing we layered for protection. Our once-spirited walk was now laden as we pushed through to our next stop. Casualties from other groups were beginning to show as wearied hikers, hunkered by rocks along the path, moaned while their guides attended to them. This was the first time we started to experience the reality that not everyone makes it. In fact, our guides had confirmed what we had read and heard: 30% of all travellers in general do not successfully summit Uhuru. We were also familiar with various blog sites stating that the Marangu route attributed greatly to this number. Sensing our drop in enthusiasm, Dismas checked in with each of us as we walked silently in single file.

"How are you doing, mama?" he asked me kindly. ("Mama" was the name I acquired on the trip, as Jessica and I were a mother/daughter team.)

"I'm good," I said, more robotically than genuinely.

"Are you feeling okay?" he prodded. "Any headaches? Stomach good?"

"Oh, yeah. I'm good," I repeated. "Just a little tired from the wind. Not much protection here."

"We will be stopping for a break soon," Dismas said reassuringly. "Do you see over there to the left?" He pointed to a small grouping of buildings and many dome tents, which seemed to appear out of nowhere.

"Is that Kibo?" I asked with new energy.

"That it is, mama. That it is." His face beamed, knowing that he had given us the mental fuel to keep our momentum strong.

The wind continued to blow relentlessly with each step. Our face covers offered some protection from the blowing red dust from the path but offered little warmth. With eyes on the mesmerizing huts in the distance, we continued our walk "pole-pole." Wishing that we could get to our destination quicker did not lessen the weight of our feet. We continued to trudge silently and robotically behind Joe.

Our lunch stop came a few moments later but was met with mixed emotions. We were ready to rest, but there was no shelter from the relentless, cold wind. We had hoped for a reprieve from the elements and wondered why we would stop here when we could see the camp so clearly ahead. Dismas explained that the camp was at least another hour of walking and that it only looked closer.

I turned up the collar on my coat and positioned my back to the strong wind. The packed lunches had always been such a pleasure. We were treated to roasted meat, buns, salad, fruit, cookies, and drinking boxes. However, looking into my boxed lunch was anything but comforting. It was hard to describe. I didn't have a headache exactly, and I wasn't sick, but I had absolutely no appetite. All I knew was that, since we stopped, I was overcome with chills. I checked to see how Jessica was doing. She was fairing better, nibbling on her bun and sipping on a juice box. Kathy also commented that she wasn't hungry and wanted to get moving again. Cameron had remained stoic and focused as he quietly ate. I forced myself to eat the foods that seemed the most comforting but packed the rest, untouched, and offered it to the group of porters. They were more than thankful for the additional food, and I was glad it wasn't going to waste.

An hour later found us standing inside one of the sleeping rooms in the cinderblock building, finally out of the wind but still shivering. This was Kibo, the location where all of the routes converged. It was the first time we had seen so many climbers in one place. We moved our packs into a room with 12 beds.

Joe and Dismas followed us, and Joe offered sage advice: "Try to get far from the door. It will be cold when it opens."

After settling into our bunks, I decided to make my way to the toilets. One of the side effects of the Diamox tablets was increased urination. On my way back, I saw Dismas.

He sauntered over with a big smile and asked, "See up there?"

I looked past his pointing finger to the black mountainside.

"That is where you are going to be very soon." He smiled as if he had seen the future. "This is what you came to do, and you will succeed!" He smiled and continued on his way.

I needed that. I was feeling quite tired from the six-hour trek in the wind, and the chills hadn't subsided since we had stopped for lunch. I headed back to my bunk where the rest were settling in for a quick nap before dinner. I applied Hot Paws strips to my back and torso, hoping to generate some heat to stave off the chills, layered back up, and buried myself deeply into my sleeping bag. Never had I fallen so quickly or so deeply asleep before.

In retrospect, the strategies that Dismas had implemented were the same type of strategies that successful businesspeople use to reach their goals. Leaders need to have a clear vision and ensure that every team member stays true to that vision. Leadership doesn't take a position in a line or hierarchy; leadership requires vision from all angles. That means stepping to the back at times to see the entire picture. A true leader inspires and mentors others to lead, always ensuring that the process has the potential for future growth.

Even though we all thought that we could go faster and farther at the beginning, Dismas stayed with the plan to move at a pace that encouraged progress. Leaders can get wrapped up in the glory of the goal and lose sight of how the team is coping with the process. Dismas knew his team well enough to know when to stop and when to continue.

The acclimatization phase is a very important parallel for business. Although the goal still seemed far away, stopping allowed us to appreciate how far we had come. It also allowed for a very important adjustment phase. In order to move up the mountain, we had to test our bodies by reaching a little higher and a little farther but then retreating in order to adjust to the new environment. This is the same for businesses that move too quickly or grow too large without taking time to acclimatize: They run the risk of imploding.

Change can be highly obvious but also extremely subtle. If we had not had Dismas's guidance, we may have moved too quickly. We saw the results

of not adapting to the changes with the ever-growing number of casualties along the path. Much like business, not everyone makes it to the top.

Implementation is where action creates traction!

How to Create the Implementation Phase in Your Business

The Implementation phase is a critical phase, focusing on the development and application of strategies that will build momentum. It is more than initiating action; it is the coordination of all business activities including products and service development, supply chain management, clientele growth and maintenance, staff development and incentives, and the setting and evaluation of goals for both short- and long-term planning.

This is an exciting but challenging phase of business success because it requires you to take out the ideas that have been safely tucked into your mind in order to act on them. *Don't overthink it!* The reality is that ideas can fail, but it's what you do with the facts from the failure that make the next steps meaningful. If you have been following the A.C.T.I.O.N. Plan steps, you will be better prepared for the reality of this phase. Strive for the goals and minimize any setbacks.

Progress Checklist

Awareness
- You know who you are as a business.
- You know who your client is and who it is not.
- You know how your business fits into the current market.

Commitment
- You have defined your business and have conceptualized the target you want to achieve.
- You have a business plan to guide you.

Team
- You have a team supporting your vision.

An obstacle is only an obstacle if you let it stop your progress.

You are not winging it. Be patient with the journey. This is the phase that will test your mettle. What could go wrong? The greatest success stories are riddled with challenges. You will fall down and you will have the wind taken out of your sails, but you will also weather the storms and find solid footing in order to continue. Major setbacks have plagued the best. Some famous people who experienced setbacks and failures include Walt Disney, Thomas Edison, Fred Smith (FedEx), Steve Jobs (Apple), Steven Spielberg, Colonel Sanders, and Henry Ford. The obstacles you face today will be tomorrow's building blocks—as long as you learn from them and keep going.

Evaluate challenging obstacles. You may find that they are not as immovable as you once thought, or that there is a way to get around or over them. With an eye on your goal, an obstacle may become a sturdy step on which to stand. Once you maneuver it, it becomes a part of the business landscape.

If your business is currently established, take a reading on whether it is thriving or barely surviving. The following Business Evaluation Checklist will help you determine where to focus your efforts.

Business Evaluation Checklist

Check the pulse of your business today. Indicate how your business is performing for each question presented, using a scale of 1 to 10 (1 is low satisfaction and 10 is high satisfaction).

BUSINESS PERFORMANCE	SCORE
Clear goals that are understood and supported	
Successful achievement of business goals	
Effective marketing strategy	
Effective time management skills	
Ability to attract the best employees	
Ability to develop staff to be achievers	
Ability to retain the best staff	
Customer service level	
Health of team	
Happiness and job satisfaction of staff	
Total Score: _____%	

Want to improve your rating? The following section reviews each of the 10 categories and offers options to consider implementing. As mentioned, the Implementation phase is very important. It must be stressed that your own business's implementation strategies will be unique to your needs. These points offer a launching point to apply to your situation. This is also the place where many businesses seek the advice of a business consultant to ensure they haven't missed a key step.

Clear Goals That Are Understood and Supported

To improve your rating, consider the following:
- **What:** Create clear goals.
- **How:** Review your mission statement. Define who your client is. Evaluate your business using the following SWOT (Strengths, Weaknesses, Opportunities, and Threats) analysis.

	STRENGTHS	WEAKNESSES
I N T E R N A L		
E X T E R N A L	OPPORTUNITIES	THREATS

From this analysis, you can begin to see key areas on which you need to focus. Goals are the main, broader category that you are wishing to achieve. They must be tangible and measurable. When a strong goal is created, supporting targets and measurable performance indicators can be established. If goals are the "what," then targets and performance indicators are the "how," with KPIs (Key Performance Indicators) being the measurement of progress.

A weakly stated business goal is to "make more money." This is intangible as you have no specifics regarding how much is required and no date by when this is to be achieved. Progress needs to be measured specifically.

A better business goal is to "increase market share annually." This is a recognized business topic that can be measured using the following calculation:

$$\text{Market share} = \frac{\begin{array}{c}\text{Company's sales} \\ \text{(over a period of time)}\end{array}}{\begin{array}{c}\text{Total sales of the industry}^{1} \\ \text{(over the same period of time)}\end{array}} \times 100$$

From here, targets can be determined to support this goal:

- **Supporting target example:** Increase overall sales by "x"% in one fiscal year.

To further support this, create KPIs that can actively measure this progress:

- **Supporting KPI example:** Increase closing ratio by "x"%, in one fiscal year, by introducing new product line "ABC" to all new leads.

---

1. Industry statistics are available through local and federal government sites.

A.C.T.**I**.O.N. PLAN

KPIs will be discussed in the section entitled "Successful Achievement of Business Goals" on page 115.

Here are some general goals and targets to start focusing on the progress of your business, starting with the following main goals examples:[2]

- Your business in the marketplace (market share placement)
- Sales goals (department targets, individual targets, number of closes/ leads, overall $/client, product type/# of client, time-to-close rate)
- Production/service goals (purchase-to-delivery timelines, # of deliveries/ day, deficiency rate)
- Team goals (department goals, service ratings)
- Client goals (customer numbers, satisfaction ratings, product/client demographics)
- Philanthropy goals (supporting community)

Here are some target examples to consider:

- Increase market share by …
- Improve return on investment by …
- Lower production costs by …
- Increase marketing plan effectiveness by …
- Increase staff support by …
- Increase customer service effectiveness by …
- Establish a philanthropic engagement by …

In a manufacturing and delivery business, targets should speak to efficiencies relating to transportation (cost and time), inventory management, logistics, client wait time, internal overproduction and overprocessing (too many hands touching the product before delivery), known deficits, and maximizing skills of the team. Many of these points are relevant to any business, but manufacturing processes add an

---

2.   This is not a complete list of options, but it should give you a start to consider what your business focus is.

additional layer to the implementation process that must be observed to be efficient.

A major consideration you must ask yourself before you commit to a goal is, "What difference will this make to my business, and is it measurable?" A goal is useless if it can't be measured. The questions of how much, how fast, and by when are examples of measurement attributes to attach to a goal.

Create an Interactive Process for Goal Development

Creating goals, targets, and KPIs are essential for the success of your business. They are not, however, destined to sit in a written form. They are intended to incite action. Here are some examples of how to start to put your goals into action:

- Gather your data by asking the following questions: What are your monthly, quarterly, and annual targets? What are your team members' responsibilities, and when and how are they expected to produce results?
- Communicate with your team. Conduct weekly progress meetings as well as quarterly department meetings, and allow for spontaneous interaction that fosters team support.
- Act on what you learn. Employ a "call-to-action" format (i.e., what is to be done, by whom, and by when). Conduct performance reviews to ensure that your team understands their responsibilities and check how they are progressing as a team member. Starting with the big picture (long-term goals), define what you would like to achieve in two to five years and after. It is never too early to describe what you would like your exit strategy to look like. Your short-term goals will define what you expect to achieve annually, quarterly, monthly, weekly, and daily.

- Write down your goals, and share them with those who will make them happen.

Successful Achievement of Business Goals

As I mentioned in the previous point, goals are not intended to sit as a written document; they require action to be meaningful.

- Review your team. Do you have the right number of the right people doing the right things? Usually, one of these three checkpoints will highlight a problem that needs to be rectified. Be aware that people in teams often need an adjustment phase if they are new, so make sure your targets are not too lofty. New employees need to know the goals they are expected to achieve but should have smaller targets moving them toward the ultimate goal.

- Investigate the value of a computer system and specialized programs, which allow you to obtain relevant information quickly such as comparing year-to-date stats to previous years on any given point of interest. Compare quarters and track seasonal impacts. Add notes to explain your results. For example, "Local sports team was in the playoffs and less traffic in the store" tells you that your clients may be sports fans. Use that information for the following year rather than expecting to listen to cricket chirps when the season rolls around.

- Employ a follow-up process to strengthen your business relationships and build a strong referral base. Clients like to know you care, or they will soon forget they did business with you. Don't be a one-hit wonder. Ensure that your team can cultivate appropriate leads in order to meet your targets.

- Create KPIs in order to measure the progress you are making toward your goals.

A.C.T.I.O.N. PLAN

Develop Strong KPIs

If you are going to spend resources on the development of KPIs (and you should definitely develop KPIs for your business), they need to follow an effective criterion. Most businesses follow the "SMART" process for developing effective KPIs:

- **S (Specific):** It should be obvious what the KPI is measuring and how the measurement will be achieved.
- **M (Measurable):** Results can be presented as a tangible value.
- **A (Achievable):** The indicator must be achieving something in which the business is engaged.
- **R (Relevant):** The indicator is measuring something that is important to achieving the target of the goal.
- **T (Time):** Is there a time limit or deadline for retrieving the data?

The following are examples for ease of explaining the process. The process works the same with goals that are much loftier.

Business: Happy Healthy Fruit Farm

Goal: To achieve $1 million in sales within the next fiscal year

Targets: $1,000,000 / 12 = $83,333.33 per month (round your values to the most logical value)

Specific targets might be percentage of specific product sales:

> 50% of sales from blueberries
>
> 30% of sales from strawberries
>
> 20% of sales from blackberries

You could then assign dollar targets to each fruit for a yearly goal and for monthly targets. If you have historical data, you can set the monthly targets to respond to seasonality. The KPIs that would be associated with these targets would assist in identifying if you are on track to meeting your targets and ultimate goal.

If your historical data tell you the volume of berries sold per month and the quantity that is typically purchased by a client, you can begin to develop forecasted sales expectations. Further, if you were anticipating growth, you would develop measurable KPIs that would assist you in reaching your target (e.g., determining the number of clients required to achieve the new target, reduction in spoiled fruit before delivery, and new target markets to address expanded application).

If goals are the "what," KPIs are the "how."

Developing and tracking KPIs to support targets help the company's decision makers as well as the individual salesperson. If results fall short of the targeted sales, actions or adjustments can be made to correct any downfalls. Alternatively, when sales exceed expectations, the company can be proactive with this information to ensure that they are prepared to meet the new demands.

Effective Marketing Strategy

Developing a marketing strategy is an important step in the success of your business. It requires you to hone your awareness skills because, when you hit the mark accurately, your efforts will build traction and momentum. The keys to creating an effective approach can be summed up as follows:

Awareness + Timing = Relevance

Relevance is paramount for successful marketing. If the idea is good but before its time, it won't hit the mark. If you know that *now* is the time to act but you're not ready, you will miss that window of opportunity and arrive too late at the party. Hopefully, this won't be your only party invitation, and you will be ready in the future. It is critical to be aware of your company's goals, what your clients' needs are, and what your staff can deliver as well as external influences (such as the economy) and the industry performance in general.

The following section will assist you in making the best decisions for your business.

THE TRIAD OF BUSINESS DECISIONS

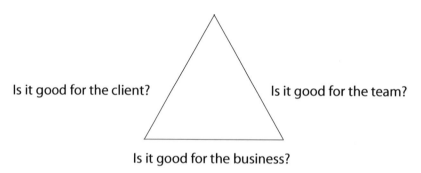

Regardless of whether you plan to market your business on your own or whether you engage the assistance of a marketing specialist, you need to do your homework:

- Refer to your mission statement.
- Review who your client is.
- Have your stats available, with notes indicating what impacted the results.
- Using an 18-month rotating calendar, which allows you to plan in advance, indicate all activities you know of and place them on the calendar. Include activities that have direct as well as indirect impact on your business. Indirect activities can launch business opportunities and new partnerships. Once activities are noted, start

to plan your advertising campaign to take advantage of these set activities. Computer programs are excellent for setting up long-term and recurring events and activities. They are also effective for sharing calendar information between departments for coordinated events as well as keeping long-distance partners up to date with activities. This is particularly useful for businesses with multiple locations.

- Track results of advertising efforts and make adjustments along the way.

W.I.N. Model for Successful Client Development

The W.I.N. Model is a three-step acronym that focuses on the phases of a business-client relationship. All businesses—even the most successful—had to start with a new client. Regardless of where your business is in its life cycle, attaining and maintaining clients are some of the most valuable processes you will want to develop.

- **W (Window Shopping):** This is a metaphor for capturing the attention of your client. Like a well-displayed store window, clients have the opportunity to decide whether they see something they like or whether they will walk by. When creating a window-shopping experience, consider location, location, location. How will you find your clients, and

If your business display is interesting, clearly showcases your product or service, and is in a location where your intended client can find it, you would expect that your "window" would attract the right clients.

A.C.T.**I**.O.N. PLAN

how will your clients find you? The window is simply a metaphor for business being present and accessible to a target market.

* Is your business a physical site?
* Is your business website and Internet based?
* Does your business stand out or get lost with the competition?
* Can your client tell what you do?
* Is your presence relevant or dated?

THE W.I.N. MODEL CHECKLIST
What am I displaying?
Is it capturing the attention of my intended audience?
Is the presentation of my product or service well displayed and defined?
Is my offering relevant and updated to capture new business?
Am I positioned where new clients can find me?
Do I have a tracking method to determine how effective my window display is for converting prospects into clients?

When creating a digital, web-based process, ensure that you are using keywords that search engine optimizers can recognize so that your business can easily be found during Internet searches.

- **I (Ideal Client):** Once the client moves past your "window display," you engage in a dialogue. This dialogue is an exchange of what a client is looking for and what you provide. The critical point of this interaction focuses on whether or not there is a fit. Businesses need to be particularly critical during this interaction.

  Remember: You cannot be everything to everyone. Do not be afraid to say "no" to a client. It will save time, money, and emotional anguish in the future! However, if you are focused on what your business is and who your target client is, you will have the proper footing to create a solid foundation for a business relationship.

  These characteristics become the benchmark to strive for when engaging new clients. You will experience slips in judgment from time to time; even the most focused businessperson will sway from

Climb Your Mountain

✓ Define your ideal client. _____

_____

_____

✓ List three of your best clients. _____

_____

_____

_____

✓ Indicate why they rated highly. _____

_____

_____

_____

✓ Look for commonalities among your selections. _____

_____

_____

_____

A.C.T.**I**.O.N. PLAN

their better judgment and get "seduced" by a potential sale or deal. However, the wise businessperson learns from these experiences and does not repeat the error, admitting that they didn't listen to their "gut" or say "no" to a feeling they had. The more focused you are on your target market and understand how you can serve them better, the more successful your business will be.

- **N (Networking):** The "N" stage refers to the network of referrals that builds from a single client. This allows you to grow your business with the most powerful tools: a satisfied customer and a supportive testimonial. These referrals bring the process back to the window-shopping phase, and the process builds momentum. When the Networking stage steps in, you will see major growth in your business. This word-of-mouth process can go viral, telling everyone about your product and service. Be prepared!

  The Networking stage is a natural progression once the ideal client has been identified. When you look critically at the Ideal Client stage, you will likely think of where these clients can be found. This may prompt you to join associations or social programs that will allow you to naturally engage them. When you connect with your ideal clients, you can trust their comments to help you develop your products and services, beyond what you currently offer.

The W.I.N. Model is a fundamental process for both new and established businesses. There is always a need to inject fresh, new clients into the mix in order to ensure growth and sustainability. Implementing the W.I.N. strategy will assist you in maximizing your market plan.

Another important strategy to implement early on in a business's life cycle is mastering time management techniques.

Effective Time Management Skills

There are many seminars and courses in which you can enroll your staff; however, unless they have support to stick to their new process, they will revert back to ineffective work practices. Help keep your teams on track by providing goals and incentives.

Whatever you and your team act on (or don't act on) will have consequences. Results follow a simple formula:

$$\frac{\text{Action}}{\text{Time}} = \text{Results}$$

The best time to ask for a referral is when your client is thrilled with your performance.

However, do not be fooled into thinking that the results in this formula are the ones you are striving for. These could be the results you want or even those you do not want. If results are low and action or effort appears great, your team is busy but not effective. If time remains constant (i.e., the same number of working hours in a day) and results are great, then the effort is likely being effectively applied. Simple, right? Yet this is a step that many businesses fail to monitor. They do not define the results expected and fail to support effective action.

Help your team track results. Everyone needs to know the company's overall goal and how their individual targets support it. Here are some points that can help your sales team monitor their progress:

- Take your annual sales target, and translate it into monthly and weekly goals. (Take into consideration relevant seasonal peaks and valleys.)
- Consider how much of the business may come from repeat business and where you will attract new business.
- Monitor your activities.
- Look for trends and opportunities to maximize your results.

Time Stealers

Over the years, I have been asked to present on many topics, and the most popular topics have related to the enigma of time management. From those seminars, here are three time management strategies to implement now:

1. **Catch and Release:** We know that business is not black and white. As I mentioned before, it is personal. Although it is important to appreciate and respect the humane side of business, it is equally important to provide a process to manage emotions because emotions can either elevate performance or diminish it. Personal baggage brought to work or a confrontation with a coworker, boss, or client can breed fear, anger, resentment, or envy that can stop you and your team from reaching your goals. When you find emotions sabotaging your effectiveness, practice the following:
   - Breathe, slowly and deeply. I know it sounds trite, but there is a great deal of scientific merit to this action. Taking a deep breath slows down your heart rate. Our body has two nervous systems: the autonomic and the sympathetic. As the names imply, the autonomic makes everything run without us being consciously aware of its activities. The sympathetic, on the other hand, responds to our reactions of the world around us. It kicks in when you jam on the brakes when a cat dashes across the road

in front of you and gives people that jolt of power in an emergency. In short, it is the system that reacts to our emotions. It senses danger and responds by setting into motion a variety of bodily activities. It cranks up our heart rate so that blood is pushed to our muscles (in case you need to make a run for it), reverts to a shallow and quicker breathing pattern, and secretes a high-test hormone into our system called "adrenaline." This is all great if you were actually in danger; however, it is counterproductive if you are simply emotional and need a calm, rational approach to get through the moment. The shallow breathing makes less oxygen available to your brain and triggers the release of new red blood cells, making the heart work harder. All in all, the result is an emotional, nervous confrontation. Breathing slowly (in through your nose and out through your mouth) actually reduces these uncomfortable feelings. It doesn't make the confrontation go away, but it changes your body's path, enabling you to react in a more effective manner.

- Stick to the facts. If you don't have facts to back your story, get them. Remind the person whom you are dialoguing with that you intend to stick to facts.

Time management is not about saving time; it is about using the time you have in the most effective manner to get the best results.

- Listen with the intent to resolve the situation. You can see how hard this would be if you let your sympathetic nervous system take over. While you listen, search the dialogue for what really happened. Sometimes the result will be a simple misunderstanding that can be cleared up with an explanation. If action needs to be taken, do so—calmly and methodically. If you messed up—own it. In all situations, these are great learning opportunities, so frame your dialogue to reflect that goal.

- It is highly likely that the other individual will not have the advantage of knowing how to implement this technique and will likely be highly emotional. You can guide the conversation. Show that you are in control. Write down the facts or concerns and indicate that you will follow up on the situation. Do so, and get back to them in a timely manner—with facts.

- Apologize if it is warranted, act to rectify the situation, and learn from the experience.

- Move on.

It is one thing to say that you expect your team to act responsibly; it is quite another to position yourself as an example. Acting as a leader, in managing emotions, is the first step in effectively mentoring your team to desired results. Knowing that your team reacts well under pressure and can deal with unexpected situations effectively will be critical for a successful reputation. Catch what is important from the experience, and release all the other stuff. *Try* it. It works! This is equally effective in your personal life as in your business life.

2. **411 vs. 911:** Do you find that people constantly interrupt you in your day and, as a result, you can't seem to get anything done? In order to manage your time successfully, set parameters for yourself as well as those around you. This 411-911 system is part

of a seminar I present entitled "The Art of Delegating" and is a coaching point that is requested frequently.

This process simply puts information into two categories: Nice to Know and Needs to Know. A 411 rating implies that the action can be scheduled for another time; a 911 rating implies, "Stop everything. This needs to be dealt with now!" The trick is to communicate your system to those around you. What seems urgent to another team member may in fact not be urgent to your day. Educate your team, and you will help them be more efficient with their own time as well.

411 VS. 911	
911 Info You Need to Handle	911 Info Someone Else Needs to Handle
411 Info You Need for Later	411 Info Someone Else Needs for Later

This is a great exercise to practice if you are having a hard time firing yourself from activities that others should be doing. If you train your team to come to you with everything, you will be sabotaging your business's success. Coach your team to evaluate situations as they experience them. Mentor toward the development of solutions before they come to you. Ultimately get them to exercise the process of knowing when to bring in assistance and when to share information. There are definitely times when you, as an owner, need to be involved and informed immediately, which should be your primary training for your team. Once those parameters are identified and understood, other situations can be categorized into the quadrants effectively.

3. **The 20-Minute Rule:** This is my favourite tool because I can be a procrastinator. Procrastination is a major culprit when it comes to mismanaged time. My clients, my family, and I all use this process because it is universally applicable. Procrastination happens to all of us. Although I do not have proof, I wouldn't be surprised if Albert Einstein or Michelangelo succumbed to the weight of procrastination from time to time. The 20-Minute Rule is a simple and effective technique that helps you get started, which is the crux of the dilemma. Why 20 minutes? It seems to be an agreeable amount of time in which people are willing to engage, making an avoidable task more bearable. The process allows a large project to be broken down into manageable 20-minute pieces.

Here are some situations that people avoid:
- Writing a report
- Doing follow-up paperwork
- Organizing a work space
- Making a difficult call
- Completing an expense report

The list is endless and can be quite personal. The 20-Minute Rule works on the premise that you need something to get you started. All you need are the items related to getting the task accomplished (e.g., phone, files, computer, pen/paper, and timer—a cell phone alarm works well). Agree to work toward accomplishing your goal and to not check the time. Set the timer and begin.

Here's what you will experience:
- You finished the task that has been holding you back; or
- You got started on a task to the point you can continue at a newly scheduled time. (This is noted when you spend 20 minutes organizing yourself for a major task, such as report writing or doing your income tax); or

- You got started, you feel the momentum, and you decided to continue.

I've seen this work for students as well as for business leaders. You just need to commit to 20 minutes and experience the momentum.

Ability to Attract the Best Employees

Just as an award-winning recipe can become a dismal flop with inferior ingredients, so can a business when the wrong people are employed. Attracting the right people is not as difficult as one might think, particularly if you have been following the processes offered in the A.C.T.I.O.N. Plan so far. If you have paid attention to creating a place where people want to work, half of the mountain has already been climbed. Knowing what you're looking for will definitely improve your chances at finding the right fit.

Here are some points to consider for finding great employees:

- You will often find the best employees already working.
- Look for individuals who have transferable skills (e.g., a great waiter may have the skills you need in sales, customer service, or marketing). Job knowledge can often be taught, but skills are inherent. You can teach an individual how to use a software program, but they may not have the people skills to converse effectively with the sales team or customers.
- Ask your referring partners if they know people who might be a good fit for your business.
- A placement agency may provide a great group of candidates from which to select. When you work with a talented recruiter whom you trust, you can build your team quickly.

- You can always follow the traditional approach to finding staff by placing an ad. Regardless of how you find possible hires to fill important team roles, *do your homework, and check their references*!

The Implementation phase requires you to coordinate the four pillars of your team. Review their purposes, and hire according to your business's needs and life cycle.

1. **Visionary:** Are you requiring someone to help you hone your idea and create a tangible target that allows you to imagine achieving its success in the future? Do you need someone who has diversified experience to infuse insight that your business has not yet experienced? Do you need visionary expertise in a specific department that is more specialized than your skills provide?

2. **Strategist:** Do you require someone who can coordinate many departments to create a roadmap to move your business forward effectively? Are you developing a middle management team to spearhead departments independently yet has the ability to collaborate in order to achieve the business's ultimate goals? Is your business stuck because, although it can maintain the status quo, it struggles to move forward?

3. **Implementer:** Do you require more hands on deck to make your targets a reality? Have you expanded your reach, requiring more talent to fill positions to ensure that customer service is exceeded?

4. **Evaluator:** Does your business create copious amounts of data, yet you are unable to acquire answers to important business questions effectively and efficiently? Have you been making major decisions without having hard data to support your actions? Have you let opportunities pass by because you did not have data to allow you to act on them in a timely manner?

Think like a successful business owner.

Remember: When you are confident and committed, you will attract the right people.

Ability to Develop Staff to Be Achievers

Once you have hired the right team members, it is imperative that you act in a responsive and proactive manner in order to develop them as team leaders. By providing relevant training, compensation, and opportunities, your team members will support the business's goals because this is the place they want to be.

Here are some suggestions on developing your team to be effective achievers:

- Develop or review your incentive plan. Ensure that it is fair and reasonable or your team will lose interest in it and feel that the leadership is out of step with the staff and the company's reality.
- Delegate responsibilities in order to grow your team. You can't do it all, so delegate wisely. Demonstrate and mentor toward the desired outcomes.
- Discover the keys that motivate your team, and engage in activities that pique their interest. If your team has a competitive spirit, engage in fun challenges that build team spirit while delivering results.
- Send staff on seminars to develop their skills and knowledge base, or bring in subject experts to expand their knowledge.
- Purchase books, magazines, and additional resources that help your team gain competitive advantage in the marketplace.
- Ensure that annual reviews include a growth and development component, and provide regular mentoring moments that allow for recognition and support to meet these goals.
- As the company achieves its goals, make rewards greater (e.g., offer a team trip that mixes education, strategy development, team building, and fun). If possible, just send them for the fun of it, with no strings attached.

- Establish productive meeting agendas that allow your team to be aware of current situations and demonstrate how their roles impact the bottom line.

Ability to Retain the Best Staff

Once you have them, know how to keep them.
- Know what motivates your team, observe them, and ask them.
- Never ignore your team's efforts while you are dealing with challenges and fires. Challenge the overachievers, but reward them. Consider team members owning shares in the business. Let them reap the rewards of their efforts.
- Know that money is rarely the reason people leave. Focus on ensuring your business's culture as the best working environment possible.
- Each individual needs:
  - Recognition for their efforts
  - Appropriate challenges with realistic goals to feel like they are making a difference
  - Autonomy to make decisions within the scope of their role and expertise. Remember to fire yourself—at the correct time.
  - Fun in the workplace. It is imperative to lighten up the heavy workload. Watch for these warning signs: changes in health (more requested sick time), changes in personality (more preoccupied than usual), and reduction in job effectiveness (decrease in tangible productivity). These are signs of stress and could be the result of the business's environment that you have developed.
- Establish an environment rich in effective communication. Set parameters for meetings that will allow the coordination and

sharing of ideas between the pillars. By allowing your team to do what they do best and to strengthen natural skills, you will gain momentum and traction as you collectively implement the strategies for success.

Customer Service Level

The client decides if you are worth sharing their contacts with or worth complaining to their contacts about.

There may be a number of reasons why a customer service score is low:

- Team members may not be clear about who your client is and who it is not. You cannot be everything to everyone; therefore, your goal should never be to satisfy everyone. However, your team can offer alternatives to the client, which would maintain a customer-focused result. Although they may not be your clients today, they may need your services at another time and, at the very least, they may be influencers that network with your potential clients.
- There may be a discrepancy in what clients think they *should* be getting and what your business *actually* provides. Equip your team with knowledge and tools to correct any misconceptions.
- You may have been providing service that is more convenient for your business than it is for your client. Before you say "no" or "it can't be done," develop your team to think in terms

of possibilities. These solutions will set you above the crowd in the eyes of your clients.

- You haven't reviewed your suppliers regularly. I suggest quarterly reviews to monitor their products and determine how they impact your business. Always check with your clients to ensure that expectations are being met. If you sense a concern, act on it immediately.

- You may not have relied on facts. When faced with an unsatisfied customer, rely on the facts to guide you. Your customer requires a sympathetic ear, but your team requires your support. Make sure any conflict is resolved quickly and effectively for all parties. Many times, these are great teaching moments that can build relationships.

- Concerns may have been ignored. Act swiftly on all concerns; they don't go away by ignoring them. Before you act, always gather the facts and employ the three time management strategies: Catch and Release, 411 vs. 911, and the 20-Minute Rule.

- If your team is overpromising and underdelivering, initiate corrective action immediately and provide retribution to the customer.

- Is the written and verbal message provided to the client correct and clear, including warranty and return policies?

- Ensure that your follow-up procedure includes customer satisfaction.

- Ensure that your team is clear on the policies, practices, and parameters of your business, but instill flexibility within the customer experience, encouraging your team to take on a "can do" approach.

- Develop a customer appreciation program.

- Use (with permission) testimonials from real clients, and share them on your website and in promotional materials.

- Send thank-you cards to clients as well as suppliers and referring partners. People like to know that you appreciate their role in your success.

Health of Team

A healthy team is productive; the alternative is costly.
- Check your benefits package. Look into programs that are appropriate for your business.
- Provide access to stress and mental health programs.
- Offer a subsidy for team members wishing to join a fitness program.
- Encourage suggestions from the team, and be prepared to make changes to the business practice if it can reduce stress and encourage fun and productivity. Ideally, the change would also result in a great improvement to the bottom line because a healthy, productive team will deliver the bottom line more effectively.
- An effective leader recognizes the health of individuals in a team and swiftly acts to improve conditions when necessary.

Happiness and Job Satisfaction of Staff

If you have focused on improving the first nine points from the Business Evaluation Checklist, then happiness and job satisfaction will likely follow. When you develop your business with an appreciation for your team, you will create an atmosphere of support. Studies show that money is not the #1 reason that staff leave their employ but rather the lack of appreciation, unresolved work stress, unclear expectations, lack of structure or strategies to be successful, and limited vision for growth opportunities. Another key ingredient to job satisfaction is to have fun. Working to be successful is hard, so take time to lighten the mood and enjoy the experience along the way. By focusing on the previous points, business owners will build the foundation of a happy, healthy team that will proudly support efforts to achieve goals.

" *Leading a healthy, motivated team is much more effective than the alternative.* "

In Summary

Review and set your major goals annually, using quarterly and monthly reporting periods to determine whether you are on course or whether you need to adjust your sails. The following five steps to goal setting will guide your progress and help you to achieve attainable results.

1. Think BIG: Take a big-picture view of the complete situation. In order to develop annual and future goals, you need to look to the horizon. Work with a 12- or 18-month calendar.
2. Consider your business (what you have):
    *   What are your services?
    *   What are the costs of these services?
    *   What new services or processes do you plan to include in the future?
    *   When do you plan to see these services implemented?
    *   What will they cost your company?
    *   Who will develop, implement, and evaluate their execution?
    *   What staff needs to be hired and trained for key roles?
    *   By what time do you wish to see results? Include key achievements/goals on your calendar to establish timelines.
    *   What are your costs on an annual, quarterly, and monthly basis?
3. Consider your personal goals (what you need):

- Look at your lifestyle and personal expenditures. Take a look at a full year's worth of expenses to ensure that you are not missing a seasonal or an annual expenditure.
- Be prepared to adjust your personal spending, if needed, to reflect your business's stage of development.
- Identify your business's break-even point, with creditors paid on time, at the various growth stages, and create strategies that allow you to invest back into the business while paying yourself as well.
- Consider what you need at the end of the first year, and then forecast what you will need for the next two to five years.

  Do not set your targets too high so that their achievements are unreachable. In the same spirit, do not limit your goals to a level below what you can achieve.
4. Consider the following points when developing your future business targets:
   - The stage of your business (established vs. startup)
   - Client development (current and prospective growth)
   - Product and service development (maintenance and diversification of your lines)

You will get where you plan to (or not plan to) go.

- Staffing complement (your current and future requirements)
- Seasonality of the business (what you can offer or implement to minimize downtime)
- Market saturation and price point influences

Once you have clearly identified the cost of running your business, and you can forecast what your business can produce in the first year, you can begin to make reasonable projections. The best strategies to implement, in order to achieve your targets, are to establish KPIs. Consider your goal to be your summit: the peak of success. Although it is off in the distance, it guides you and keeps you focused. Targets are smaller plateaus along the way. They keep you motivated to continue to strive for the summit. KPIs are measurements to ensure that your targets are accurate. KPIs are the ultimate "how" that validates the "what" of the targets in order to successfully achieve the goal.

5. Implement the "W.I.N. Model for Successful Client Development" on page 119 as a guide to develop a relevant marketing strategy. Your goals and targets will only be successfully achieved if your business is properly presented.

- What are you providing that will attract new business?
- Can you find your clients? Can they find you?
- Add value to your customer service plan.
- Know who your client is, and diligently offer solutions.
- Build on your existing clients. Show your appreciation for their loyalty, and strengthen business ties.
- Maintain and grow your client base through effective networking.

Think of your financial goals. Your business is not a charitable organization; it's intended to be a profitable and viable venture. When businesses start out or plan for major growth, financial assistance may be required. The Implementation phase is the heartbeat of the business as it engages the creative process that melds purpose with need, setting the stage for successful strategy development. Invite experts to share their knowledge to improve your systems and processes, and take time to expand your personal knowledge by researching best practices that will build traction in your business. You will always be faced with making decisions. At times you will experience challenges as to which decision to act on first and which strategy to implement over another. In a democratic business that fosters independent thinkers, you will likely have lively debate about the direction you should choose. How can you make sure that your team stays focused? *Simply by reminding them why your business exists and what your big-picture goal is.* Implementing "The Triad of Business Decisions" on page 140 will guide you and your team to make effective decisions that support the business goals.

Plan to thrive and not merely survive.

Note that "Is it good for the business?" is situated at the base of the triangle for a reason. If it's not good for the business, move on to an alternative strategy. Clearly, the best approach is to never let any one side of the triangle become disproportionate to the goals. Stick to facts, and leave emotions outside for the moment. Give equal time to all opinions and *consider those options that can be measured.*

To effectively lead your team through the Implementation processes:

- Look at the big picture.
- Break it down into reasonable steps.
- Create goals with timelines.

THE TRIAD OF BUSINESS DECISIONS

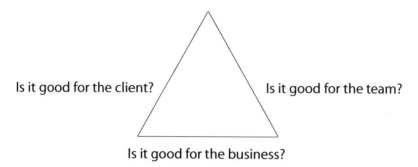

Is it good for the client?

Is it good for the team?

Is it good for the business?

- Keep your team accountable.
- Focus on being consistent.
- Have fun!

Implementation requires that the Awareness, Commitment, and Team phases be engaged. As you begin to implement strategies, you will begin to feel your business's momentum. Do not let the numbers and goals intimidate you. You have a supportive team to keep you focused with the facts and ready to help you readjust if you need to. All the signs to be successful are around you. Learn how to read them, and implement your strategies to maximize traction.

Choose to be consistently successful
rather than successfully consistent.

Implementation
Business
Strategy

Implementation
Interview with
Dianna Bowes

https://goo.gl/RLY6FX
(time 24:05)

https://goo.gl/3O9X0j
(time 21:38)

Using a scan app, scan the QR code above, or use
the above link to access the sound file.

Note: Please allow a few moments for the file to open on your device.

A.C.T.I.O.N. PLAN

CHAPTER 5

Opportunities

While the overall goal was to successfully summit Kilimanjaro with my daughter Jessica, we saw an opportunity to accomplish even more, raising over $3,000 to support multiple sclerosis research and education. Paul Semchuk was our inspiration as we carried his photo on the journey.

Lessons from the Mountain ...

When you plan for a major adventure, like climbing Mount Kilimanjaro, one might think, "Well, that's enough to deal with," and I would agree—to an extent. We did a great amount of research, particularly at the beginning of the process. But, as we got comfortable with assembling our team, namely the people of Good Earth Tours, we experienced freedom from the details. We wanted to experience success, so we hired experts whom we trusted. We were still very much involved, but it became more of an approval role, selecting from options rather than creating from a blank slate.

This process freed up valuable time to ask the question, "What other opportunities are waiting for us to take?" The first opportunity we identified had social implications connected to a cause that was very close to my heart. My daughter Jessica and I had volunteered at a local multiple sclerosis (MS) bike fundraiser earlier in the spring. It was a two-day event where participants cycled 90 kilometers (56 miles) in one direction, stayed overnight, and then cycled back. The event was well supported, with cyclists raising significant money, individually, for the cause. This got us thinking about how our personal goal of summiting Mount Kilimanjaro might be a fundraising opportunity as well.

After contacting the MS head office, we registered as an official individual fundraising event. Until we thought of asking, we had no idea that this was an available option to consider. We set up an official MS fundraising web page called Conquer the Mountain (MS being the mountain). We described our plans to summit Mount Kilimanjaro in a few weeks and raise money in support of our local MS chapter. We were guaranteed that all donations would be used to support the local medical and educational programs in our area.

We had a personal reason for choosing this organization. My brother-in-law Paul had contracted MS several years ago. He had been a sports guy all of his life, playing on high school teams and then later, with his own family,

A.C.T.I.**O.**N. PLAN

had coached community basketball. In a few short years, MS had completely altered his path. Through shear resilience and determination, he and his supportive family (his amazing wife Carol and kids Adam and Katherine) took on the challenge to conquer his mountain. I had other very special people in my life—friends and cousins who were afflicted with this disease—and Jessica and I dedicated our climb to support those who faced the daily climb that MS presented.

We posted our fundraising page on social media, connecting with friends, family, and colleagues. Within two weeks, we raised over $3,000 and had accumulated a plethora of good wishes that would help support us during the grueling final hours of our imminent challenge.

It was an opportunity well worth taking. We knew that Kilimanjaro was our personal challenge, but now we had invited many on the road with us to make a bigger ripple. Jessica and I had decided that, if Paul couldn't physically join us, we would bring him with us—symbolically. I tucked a picture of Paul into my pack the night before we left with the thought that he would be with us every step of the way.

I wasn't yet satisfied that we had exhausted our opportunities for this trip, so I connected with Baraka of Good Earth Tours and asked him what we could do when we arrived in Tanzania and Kenya. Our timelines were firmly established, and we only had a few narrow windows to create opportunities while we were there.

The first part of our trip was a three-day safari of the Masai Mara, the wildlife sanctuary on the Kenyan side of the border; its counterpart on the Tanzanian side is the Serengeti. On the evening of our last day at the Mara Sopa Lodge, on the majestic Masai Mara, our guide brought us to the village of the Masai people. We were amazed at their hospitality, resourcefulness, and genuine contentedness.

The Masai are a proud and strong people. The women were the architects and entrepreneurs of the village. We watched a new dung hut being constructed as well as the preparation of their artisan works for market.

There was genuine curiosity as to what they could do to enhance their wares to attract the North American tourist.

One of the most memorable experiences of the visit was when the chief guided us into his home. There were no windows in the building, and the only light came from the narrow entrance that twisted and turned, making our walk based on trust rather than on sight. In the darkness, the chief spoke to us about the culture and how the village existed. The ages of the tribe ranged from two months to 94 years old, an impressive statistic for any culture. Children and women were all educated, travelling to nearby towns to schools, which he admitted was a relatively new concept.

As he spoke, our eyes adjusted to the darkness. To our surprise, we were not alone. There were many rooms adjoining the one we were seated in. Two people were resting on a bed in the corner; two more, completely unbeknown to us, sat directly in front of us, quietly listening to our conversation.

We were humbled by the experience, enjoying their display of ceremonial dances and ability to create fire in seconds. They were proud of their heritage, and they knew who they were. There were definite signs of First-World influences, such as the acceptance of education and the abundance of cell phones. (We heard that there are more cell phones in Africa than there are toilets!) These and other influences would no doubt change this civilization in the future, but I was thankful to have had the opportunity to actually experience it firsthand.

When we were leaving the village, the chief walked us to the road, which led back to our lodge. He bowed his head, held out his hand, and said, "Thank you for not judging or trying to change us."

Those words left me speechless. Living in a country of plenty where any comfort can easily be found, it is a staggering difference to see a group of people living with minimal conveniences and being profoundly happy. This was an educational experience that I would hold near to my heart. Opportunities are not always loud with massively impactful results. They can come in small, unexpected packages that influence common dialogue

A.C.T.I.**O**.N. PLAN

and build trusting relationships. That dialogue and experience were very impactful for me, and I carry them every day in business and in life. Listening with an open mind yields rich and trusting relationships.

Our third major opportunity came after we left Kenya for the Tanzanian city of Arusha. We had arrived at our accommodation, Planet Lodge, a few days before Kathy and Cameron would join us, with the hopes of taking in some day trips at higher altitudes in preparation for our climb. We had spent a great deal of our last few days in a safari vehicle, observing the amazing wildlife of the Mara Masai, and we knew that we needed to challenge our body. We had connected with a local guide who arranged for a hiking trip just outside the town.

The lush vegetation was spectacular. Our guide Baraka Luca (we soon became aware of how common this first name was) pointed out each plant and its unique qualities with expertise. As we climbed through the grassy mountain terrain, we could see an impressive mountain peak in the near distance. I could tell that it wasn't Kilimanjaro due to its peak, but it was grand. Baraka informed us that it was Mount Meru, a live volcano that last erupted in 1910. He also informed us that, with its elevation of 4,565 meters (14,978 feet), it was 1,330 meters (4,363 feet) shorter than Kilimanjaro. Our sense of perspective was being tested on this excursion, but we were about to be thunderstruck by what we would experience next.

We had heard about an orphanage and a school in the area and had hoped for a tour. Through washed-out roads and winding trails, our guide brought us to an orphanage where two curious children peaked through the door of a house. We had learned that the other children who lived in the orphanage were attending school, but these two were not yet of age. The older one was a four-year-old girl. She had been the only survivor of a house fire as a baby, tragically losing all of her fingers and scarring her face and head significantly. Clad in a long skirt and hooded sweater, she pushed through the door, more curious than the younger boy, who stayed peaking behind.

A.C.T.I.**O**.N. PLAN

Along with the guide, the little girl brought us into a room that had been the original schoolhouse—a single room with large windows and a blackboard at the front. We had brought some balls to give to the children, and she picked one that had the world on it. She was most interested when we showed her where Africa was. To thank us for the gift, she sang us her rendition of "Head, Shoulders, Knees and Toes." We asked the guide what the future held for this beautiful and courageous little girl. He said that she was very bright, already fluent in three languages. She would likely stay at the orphanage—a caring environment where the children were loved and educated. He believed that she would likely attend a university some day.

There was so much to understand in this massive country. Much progress had been made and so much to consider for the future.

On our way back to our lodge, we visited the school. There were two schools built in a communal space, each with an attendance of just over 500. There was a great deal of excitement with our visit, indicated by the bright eyes and smiling, beaming faces when we walked in. We were invited to see a class in session, so we took our seats in the back row.

We were amazed at the respect and organization displayed in the class. There were four rows of five desks; at each desk sat three children, totaling 60 students in the room. The subject was math. They did not have a computer or a calculator, just a notebook and a pencil. The teacher started the session by verbally reciting a mathematical equation. The children wrote it down and raised their hands to offer the answer. Some just did the calculation in their head. When the correct answer was provided, which was the first child the teacher called on, the class went into a support cheer, much like what is shouted when teams leave a sports huddle. The teacher then asked a student to verbally test the class on the next concept. This was interesting, as the students were encouraged to lead the class. Mimicking the teacher's process, a second mathematical problem was asked, and again the hands shot up to respond. With the correct response, the whole class participated in celebrating with another cheer.

A.C.T.I.**O**.N. PLAN

When a business owner looks for opportunities, positive action starts the ball rolling. When an entire team looks for opportunities, we figure out how man can walk on the moon.

I looked at Jessica and could see that she was astonished as well. We were both university educated, and neither of us would have confidently answered those problems with that speed—at least not without a calculator. Some people might say that they were just putting on a show for us. For those neighsayers, I would remind them that our visit was not premeditated. If they just happened to have that up their sleeve, there would have been some prior coaching in order to present it so seamlessly.

In any event, we came away with a great appreciation for the people of Kenya and Tanzania. I was thankful that we took the opportunity to experience this culture personally. It was an important reminder that preconceived ideas can be highly erroneous and that technology should be used for effectiveness and not only for efficiency.

In retrospect, we could have stuck to the major focus of our trip—summiting Kilimanjaro—but challenging the idea of what other opportunities were waiting for us made our experience richer with indelibly imprinted memories. It allowed us to make a difference in the lives of others and most definitely in ours.

How to Create Opportunities in Your Business

Ideas without action are like sailing ships without wind.

Think back to that excitingly optimistic time, in the embryonic stage of the development of your business, when your thoughts may have been something like this: "Wouldn't it be great ..." or "Someday I'd love to ..." Ideas can float away like pretty balloons disappearing into the blue sky—ideas, that is, that have not been enveloped in Awareness, tested with Commitment, supported by a Team, and moved forward with Implementation.

When you follow the steps of the A.C.T.I.O.N. Plan, your ideas become reality. Once the Implementation process begins, the cogs of the business wheel will begin to move in unison:

- The visionaries share timely observations that the strategists will mold into stepping stones to support the implementers.
- The evaluators will review the process and bring back the results to the visionaries.
- The visionaries will share the results with the strategists to fine-tune.
- The implementers will have the best practices and processes available, and the process continues.

It isn't always smooth, but patience, diligence, and constant awareness will support a solid footing to weather potential missteps. You can feel the momentum of this well-oiled machine. As a business owner, you can move into the following phase, which is necessary for growth and development.

The Opportunity phase is an exciting phase. The other phases are not dull; on the contrary, each phase is positioned at a specific place in the life cycle of your business for a reason. Opportunities are around us every day, but you need to get your "ducks in a row" before you can even recognize a possibility. Opportunities have a devilish characteristic: They can appear exciting and shiny. When you allow yourself to establish a solid foundation for your business, on which the first four phases focus, you can recognize golden opportunities from the treacherous fool's gold prospects.

When you are presented with opportunities, be prepared to evaluate their worth efficiently. You don't want to wait too long, but you never want to follow a lead before you are ready. The following points offer a checklist to see if you are ready to move into the Opportunities phase effectively:

- You are not a one-person show but delegate readily. You have realized that you cannot move your business forward if you attempt to do everything yourself. By letting go of some aspects of the business, you can spend important time on developing and not merely maintaining the business.
- You have the right number of the right people doing the right things … or at least you are moving in that direction.
- Confidence in your team will grow as they embrace your goals and accept their personal roles in achieving them. Taking time to select the right people for each role, and providing them with the tools and responsibilities to execute their roles effectively, will give you the peace of mind to explore new ground.
- You have confidence that your team clearly understands your mission statement and who your client is.
- You have encouraged your team to make decisions in your absence because they are clear on their role and the mission of the business.

- The development stage of your business has allowed you the time to observe what is happening around you and how it might impact your business—or how your business might impact the world around you.
- Your mind is free to take in new observations that might otherwise have been unnoticed when you were enveloped by the daily operations of your business. You now have the time to spend on developing new prospects because you are not losing time by putting out endless fires.
- You do not need to have everything perfectly planned out before you take a step forward. You realize that waiting for things to be perfect stops any momentum from taking hold. There is no perfect time; opportunities will not wait for you. It's okay to proceed with caution, but have the courage and confidence to proceed!

All opportunities have an expiry date. Know when to act on them.

Here is the challenge: Many owners and key decision makers find this stage very difficult. It requires confidence that your team can handle their tasks without you being directly involved in every aspect of the business. You have to let your team grow. If you are going to be successful, you have to build your business with the expectation that you will experience opportunities. That means you have to be prepared to work "on" the business and not only "in" the business. It's time, as the business leader, to take on new opportunities.

A.C.T.I.**O**.N. PLAN

Change Your Routine to Experience Opportunities

Optimize Your Health

Opportunities can be realized right under our noses; however; they rarely float into an office all by themselves. In fact, they seem to materialize when we get away from the daily routine and engage in a change of scenery. Taking a break can impact your health in a positive manner, and a healthy body and team can create a healthy business, ready to get the most out of opportunities.

To be effective, get away from the daily routine by taking short breaks in the day or longer vacation time. Daily breaks provide physical advantages, such as muscle stimulation, aerobic exchange, and endorphin release, all of which support a stronger body and mind. Following through with "getting away" time is critical to a healthy business. People who run the risk of missing the signs are the ones who brag or complain that they never take a vacation. They convince themselves that the business will fall apart without them, yet they can't see their own health falling apart—which, ironically, impacts the health of their business.

If you are looking for opportunities to take you and your business to the top, you'd better have the stamina for the climb!

Solve Problems

Leaving your routine in search of opportunities allows you to seek creative solutions to existing challenges for your business. Owners need to hit the "refresh button" once in a while in order to gain a new perspective. Everyone gets stumped or hits a dry patch where they struggle to get past an obstacle. Stepping away from the routine path (just before it becomes a rut) gives you a chance to let the creative thought process evolve. If you catch yourself mulling over a problem and not getting to a solution, change your environment. A change of view can put things in perspective, and you'll see things differently.

If you don't like what you see, change your point of view.

Build Your Expert Circle

The Opportunity phase supports the concept of engaging others in meaningful, fresh dialog. This activity allows you to expand your knowledge so you can proactively deal with current and future challenges. When you get away regularly, you have the opportunity to meet new people who may provide solutions to problems. This includes problems that you didn't even realize existed. When you are fixated on the struggles in your insular business, you will likely not even be aware of important events and movements around you. Dialoguing with other business owners provides a healthy reality check to get a fresh take on current trends.

As we discussed earlier, you can't run a business successfully by yourself. As a call to action, you were directed to *fire yourself.* This applies to thinking you know everything about running a business in the world of opportunities. You can't know everything there is to know about navigating your business through the turbulent waters of today's global changes. Opportunities are there for you to act on, but you need trusted advisors to help you reach your goal.

Keep Your Knowledge Updated and Relevant

Although building a trusted circle of influence is critical, your knowledge can be enhanced by engaging in a variety of information sources including subscribing to newsletters, listening to podcasts, and connecting with relevant associations. You can't read every book on every subject. You must be selective with your time. Scheduling events, away from your daily routine, allows you to meet new people who could offer sage advice and provide connections or referrals.

You can't be an expert on everything.
You can, however, select a network of
advisory experts whom you trust.

Climb Your Mountain

✓ Attend conventions, seminars, webinars, and symposiums.
✓ Talk to others who think in terms of opportunities and strategies.

Expand Your Personal Horizons

You are the leader. Invest in yourself. Scheduled breaks allow business owners time to explore new interests that could add important diversification to their existing business model. When people go away for a break, they become open to new ideas. Look for new ways to develop a product line, or observe a trend that hints at the future client you haven't met yet. Perhaps a getaway will spark a conversation with an individual in need of everything you represent. You may not be looking for a partner, but when opportunities work their magic, possibilities become realities when you are not expecting them, such as conversations on airplanes, observations in a quaint marketplace, or a chance meeting at a restaurant. All events could be monumental, just ready to be explored and acted on. All could be poised and ready to assist you in the climb of your life. All could evaporate if you sit in your office, worried that the business can't operate without your daily presence.

All opportunities have an expiry date. Be ready to act on them.

Leaders do not hide behind excuses. They evaluate the information that is constantly surrounding them, and they act on opportunities that build confidence and momentum.

A.C.T.I.**O**.N. PLAN

Get the Most Out of Opportunities

Lead by Example

If you want to get the most out of opportunities, you have to set the example for your team. It isn't solely your responsibility to act on opportunities, but it is your responsibility to set the expectations.

If you want to lead a proactive team, you will need to show them how to be proactive by looking out for challenges and manoeuvring them efficiently. There is no place in your organization for the statement, "That's not my job."[1] If they are part of your team, part of their job is to look for opportunities.

Don't Wait ... Create!

This is my favourite discussion point when it comes to opportunities. If you are truly focused on being successful in business, then you will not wait for opportunities to come to you—you will create them. As I said earlier, opportunities have an expiry date; however, if you miss them because you were not ready (which could be legitimate because your business was not ready to take the opportunity), you can still create an opportunity yourself. Look at the signs around you:

- What do you know?
- Whom do you know?
- What need does your business fill?

---

1. This is a common quote, of unknown origin, supporting processes that deliver honest and reasonable expectations.

A.C.T.I.**O.**N. PLAN

Climb Your Mountain

✓ Guide your team to look for ways to build stronger client-business relationships. _____

_____

_____

✓ Encourage your team to explore ways to strengthen the company's brand._____

_____

_____

✓ Reward your team for identifying ways to be more efficient and recognize their efforts._____

_____

_____

When life deals you a challenge, remodel it into an opportunity.

Develop Your Business Parachute

Running a business can be exhilarating and frustrating, and those emotions can be experienced all in the same week—actually, all in the same day! The A.C.T.I.O.N. Plan is designed to give you solid footing to help you maneuver the challenges that you will definitely experience as you climb to your goals. You will need to uncover many solutions in order to move your business along.

Every business owner will face seemingly insurmountable challenges, but there is usually a way around or over any obstacle. When you step back from the situation and evaluate the facts, you will likely see that many challenges were based on something that changed, and you just weren't paying attention. Often the signs are right under our noses; however, when you wear "business blinders," you miss some glaring signs. Sometimes the challenges are created in the world around us, and sometimes we create the challenges ourselves. These often show up in business as "bottlenecks."

Many influences factor into the success or failure of a business, and every business has the potential to have at least one major bottleneck. Bottlenecks can devastate a business, particularly when they occur at a key point. They may present themselves as the sole staff member who has the knowledge to change an order once it has gone through the system; it might be a supplier who provides a "key ingredient" to your production line; it might be an outdated and overloaded computer program that is limping arduously while it processes and stores your key data.

If something were to happen to any of these people, products, or systems, the company could crash to a halt. Entrepreneurs and business owners are the biggest culprits for being the company's bottleneck as they often hold all the keys—physically and mentally—that the business needs to run. These are bottlenecks, and bottlenecks are signs that you need a parachute or a Plan B.

Hidden bottlenecks are potentially the most devastating because, like their name implies, they are hidden. As long as everything is moving along, no one sees any danger; however, too many influences out of our immediate control can have a major impact on our business. Global weather, technology, and world economics all play a role in our business opportunities. The best time to identify your vulnerable areas and create a plan to minimize any impact is when things are going well. Don't gamble on fair weather. Be aware of what you have, and safeguard it for the future. If your business practices these strategies, your business will be set to experience constant improvement and bottlenecks will emerge. By implementing efficiency strategies, bottlenecks will be identified and quickly remediated.

A.C.T.I.**O**.N. PLAN

Climb Your Mountain

Check your business over thoroughly.

✓ Look critically for bottlenecks, and make a Plan B for every one of the situations. _____

_____

_____

✓ Make sure that every position in your company has a second individual capable of taking the lead or overlapping (temporarily) into other related areas to ensure continuity of services.

_____

_____

✓ Ensure that all procedures are accessible, and delegate a "second in command" to have access to sensitive and confidential knowledge.

_____

_____

✓ Check your suppliers and the products they provide you. Be prepared for a backup plan if they experience a shortage or closure or if they are experiencing diminished standards. _____

_____

_____

The power of opportunities in the hands of a team creates exponential results.

Five Key Ways to Uncover Opportunities Now

1. Connect with reliable sources to expand your knowledge. Network with the movers and shakers, not just the thinkers and talkers.
2. Volunteer at the grass-roots level of an organization or charity.
3. Read, watch, and listen. Surround yourself with varied topics from experts, and draw from their experiences to cultivate a rich library of knowledge. Be the go-to person who others seek for advice and connections. Here are some topics to explore that will expand your knowledge, skills, and abilities:

   - History is a great teacher of our future. Names and places may change, but situations are often repeated in history.
   - Sports and war stories can provide effective metaphors from which to develop strategies and teamwork.
   - Inspirational memoirs can provide a personal boost at a critical time in your life.
   - Interests and hobbies can keep the creative juices and problem-solving skills sharp.
   - World economics and politics give us a glimpse of the bigger, global picture.

   Challenge yourself to learn something new every day. Knowledge is king when it comes to business success. The more you know, the more prepared you are to adapt when you need to—and, in this world, you always need to adapt.

4. Step out of your daily routine. Join new groups, travel, get away, and meet interesting people who think in possibilities.
5. Challenge yourself to observe your world, and bring that knowledge back to your business. Ask yourself, "How can this impact my business, and how can my business impact this opportunity?"

Incorporate these five steps, and you will begin to see opportunities that you had never noticed before and be able to act on and create opportunities as you need them.

Final Check: Should You Act on an Opportunity (or Not)?

Here are four checkpoints to determine if you should take on a new opportunity for your business:

1. What's the point? Will it make any difference or just take time and money without any real benefit?
2. Is it right for your client base? Does this opportunity specifically answer your clients' needs?
3. Is it right for your business? Listen to the voice in your gut. Is this really in your business's wheelhouse? Are you stretching outside your knowledge and competency bases? Is it a perfect fit that will naturally grow your bottom line? Will this benefit your team?
4. Can it be sustained? Do you have the resources to maintain it if it becomes successful? How can you manage the impact on your business now and in the future?

In Summary

The Opportunity phase is an exciting developmental stage of successful business growth. When you recognize that opportunities are all around you, it can seem overwhelming. Many businesses fail because they act in haste. Panic blurs their perspective. The Opportunity phase of the A.C.T.I.O.N. Plan tests your business acumen. Opportunities do have an expiry date, but acting when you are not ready can be irresponsible and result in devastation.

Business owners who follow a strategic plan have the advantage of moving in a timely fashion toward their goals. Through observation and patience, they gain business experience that allows them to truly understand their unique business. When you know your business and what it is capable of, you can assess opportunities effectively and act on them on your terms.

Since opportunities can also mean change, many business owners make the mistake of avoiding opportunities out of fear of what those changes might bring. That assessment needs to be evaluated from a factual perspective, not an emotional one. Successful business owners are not afraid of change; they embrace it. They recognize that their world is changing all the time. They can be proactive and lead with a strategic plan, or they can be reactive. There are many important reasons to experience and seek out opportunities. They rarely come looking for you. You must be proactive and prepared to get out of your routine and go where the opportunities are.

Getting out of your routine to seek opportunities has the following side benefits:

- By proactively setting out to seek opportunities, you will get away from the daily routine and pressures, which can have important health benefits. Breathing fresh air, stretching, and using your muscles help your body and mind regain its alert edge. You can recognize opportunities when you are on your game better than when you are weighted down with decisions and pressure.
- Removing yourself from the routine and occasionally experiencing a new course can provide unexpected answers to problems. Fresh experiences can be creative outlets.
- Scheduling meetings that expand your current activities allows you to experience and develop an important circle of experts whom you may not otherwise have engaged if you remained in your insular world of routine activities.

A.C.T.I.**O.**N. PLAN

- Opportunities can be present in social and networking activities. By engaging in personal development or interests, you expand your scope of insight, which could be beneficial to your business. The more extensive your personal experiences are, the more you will develop as a person—and that makes a leader worth following.

Be curious enough to ask why and brave enough to ask why not.

- Stepping out and into new activities and venturing down alternative paths provide opportunities to expand your knowledge and view on key points that you might not have considered.

In general, seeking opportunities is an important phase that engages businesses to achieve their goals through experiencing activities that set the stage for stretching farther and achieving more than they thought possible. Acting on opportunities requires owners to step off the edge. Staying in the safe zone will not keep your business unique for long, and you could soon get lost in a sea of sameness; however, stepping off a cliff could be an irresponsible act with dire consequences—unless you have a parachute. Develop your business parachute by ensuring that you have Plan Bs at critical points in your business.

Here are some examples of how you can get the most out of opportunities:

- Lead by example. Show your team how to recognize opportunities, and encourage them to get out of their routines to seek out answers to their current challenges. This is not a skill that should only be developed by a few. Build a staff of keen observers so that opportunities are experienced exponentially.

- Don't wait ... create. Just as some businesses avoid taking opportunities, others wait until the perfect one comes along. This is not necessary. Know what your business can do, and create the opportunities you need to showcase its unique offerings.

Here are four points to check if you are ready to take on an opportunity:

1. What's the point? Is this really going make a difference? Is it unique enough to garner attention?

2. Is it right for your client base? Is this something that your clients would agree is good for them?

3. Is it right for your business and team? Is this something that fits into your mission?

4. Can it be sustained? If it turns out to be a great idea, are you able to meet a flood of demand?

A challenge is only an obstacle if you let it be.

Opportunity Business Strategy

https://goo.gl/EPPhqG
(time 17:38)

Opportunity Interview with Maureen Wright and Johanne Lewis

https://goo.gl/ieGQ5C
(time 25:56)

Using a scan app, scan the QR code above, or use the above link to access the sound file.

Note: Please allow a few moments for the file to open on your device.

A.C.T.I.O.N. PLAN

CHAPTER 6

Next

After months of preparation, we successfully summited Mount Kilimanjaro. Watching the sun awaken the world was breathtaking. Once this amazing goal was successfully realized, we found ourselves literally "on top of the world." The entire experience made a great impact on us and, not surprisingly, compelled the question, "What's next?"

Lessons from the Mountain ...

This was summit day! After our six-hour, wind-chilling hike through The Saddle, the comfort of a worn mattress on a timber-frame bunk was a welcomed sensation. It didn't seem possible that I had fallen asleep, but suddenly I was being nudged awake by my teammate. I had been out for over an hour, but I wasn't feeling better. I buried my head in my hands due to the throbbing pain across my eyes, and I tried to fully connect with my surroundings. The smell of the food, although probably delicious, did not improve my appetite.

Kathy had woken just moments before with a similar headache. She responded to my grimacing facial expressions by smiling and saying, "Take this. It's already working on me."

I took the two migraine-strength Advil tablets with a cup of hot tea. She was right. Within a few minutes, my head began to feel clearer. The chills were gone, and I felt fairly rested. The team had made their way to the communal table, which sat in the middle of our room. I had apparently slept through the meal service offered to the other four tour groups that shared our space. It would explain the heavy aroma of melded food smells that hung in the room. Each tour group ate foods provided by their own cooks, and our team was the last to be served.

I knew that I needed to eat. It was crucial to have energy for the final leg of this trek. I also knew that hydration was critical and that my headache earlier was likely a symptom of not consuming enough water while crossing The Saddle. I was determined to move past the unsettling thought that my loss of appetite might be a symptom of altitude sickness. I had come to summit Kilimanjaro, not to be stopped by mild nausea. The mind games that tested my confidence were lurking in the shadows.

I was reminded of our first moments after arriving at Kibo, as we shuffled through the corridors of the cinderblock building with our packs. Upon entering the camp, we noticed more casualties, as climbers were crouched on the ground, dealing with their ailments. They were a clear reminder that this was the point where the statistics became a reality. The number of initial climbers was great when the summit was in the distance; as the trek continued, the numbers dwindled.

When we first entered our dorm room, I was pleased to be greeted by a man and woman who had arrived just ahead of us and were unrolling their packs. Their energetic demeanor was a stark contrast from the huddled climbers we passed in the hallway. He had many mountain climbs under his belt, but this was the first for his wife. After a moment of introductions and sharing of experiences thus far, the woman offered to test our blood-oxygen levels. She pulled out a pulse oximeter and placed it on her finger. While we waited for the value to appear on the screen, she explained how the device worked. Ultimately, we were looking for an oxygen value of 80% or higher. With a beep, the device displayed her result: 72. We watched as the weight of this value changed the woman from excited and confident to panicky and anxious. Maybe there was something wrong with it. Kathy tried and her results also showed values in the low 70s. Then I tried. The screen blinked 63.

The woman looked at me with concern and compassion. "Oh, I'm sure it's just acting up," and then quickly added, "The pharmacist said that it might not read accurately with cold hands."

That was it: cold hands. My hands were notoriously cold, even on a summer day. I had mildly frozen them as a teenager, and now I had Raynaud's syndrome. In response to cold, the small arteries in my fingers experience a vasospasm, disrupting the blood flow to my fingertips.

We all rubbed our hands, jumped up and down, and swung our arms wildly about—anything to get the screen to show a number that would shake this emotional cloud. I placed my finger in the sensor and waited. I mused at the situation. I had never heard of the oximeter before this. Now, without any research on my part, I was willing to trust it and the people I had just met to provide me with the sense that I could continue successfully.

A.C.T.I.O.**N.** PLAN

"What if the number is the same—or lower?" I wondered.

I aggressively pushed these negative thoughts out of my mind, but still I could hear Dismas's voice: "Not everyone makes it to the top."

My eyes were closed as I was trying to come to an emotional state of logical awareness. What did I know? I was tired from the day's hike. I was chilled. My appetite wasn't great. My head was a bit heavy. But even with all of these real, physical symptoms, I felt a deep belief that I was going to succeed—no matter what the screen said.

The beep of the meter cut through the silence, which was quickly followed by enthusiastic cheers. The screen blinked 87! The placebo effect was alive and well. Even though I had maintained that I was going to succeed regardless of the meter's results, the effect of a significant value was an emotional boost at a critical time in the climb. The feeling of contentment, after the endorphin ride of anxiety and followed by jubilation, were likely the reasons for the deep sleep I then experienced.

Now that I was emotionally and psychologically back on track, I needed to help my body get ready for the next phase. The smell of food was still not a pleasant experience. So, with trepidation, I ladled the steaming soup into a bowl and sat on my bunk to sip it. This turned out to be comfort food at its best. It may not have had all of the nutritional requirements of a meal before a climb, but it felt like a hug from the inside out, and that psychological gain could not be denied. Although our cooks had provided a wonderful variety of food to give us the nutrition we needed, I found that a second bowl of soup was my limit.

It was just before sunset, and Jessica and I decided to take in the view from Kibo. Above us the sky was a spectacular blue that almost looked like velvet. Thousands of stars punctuated the darkness over the towering mountain face that steeply rose to the west of our camp. At the top of that mountainous wall, hidden from our view, was our summit point. To the east, the sky was a stunning glow of coral and gold, a reflection of the glorious sunset. Mawenzi's castle-like silhouette stood majestically in the distance as

A.C.T.I.O.**N.** PLAN

the final remnants of light evaporated over the steep mountain wall leading to Uhuru Peak.

The sun's setting was followed by the spectacular appearance of the moon. During our research for the best time to climb Kilimanjaro, Kathy had noted that there would be a supermoon during the first week of August, and we planned our climb to have the moon guide us to our summit. "Supermoon" is the common name for the astrological positioning of the earth, the sun, and the moon, making the moon appear significantly larger and brighter than normal.

Like a halogen beacon, the supermoon had not disappointed. Standing on this magnificent precipice, and gazing off to the fading sunset at an elevation of 4,720 meters (15,485 feet), I realized how very fortunate I was. No matter how this would finally play out, the experience so far was worth it.

I'm not sure when he arrived, but I noticed Dismas standing quietly beside me, also taking in the view.

"Don't worry," he said calmly. "I've been watching you all. You are going to make it to the top."

"Yeah?" I responded, believing it too. "How do you know?"

"You are all determined. No complaints. You are strong in your body and your head." As he gazed at the horizon, he continued seriously, "And you have me." Then his serious expression changed into a broad grin.

"Yes, we do," I agreed. "Yes, we most certainly do!"

Now that the sun had set and the night sky had covered us like a blanket, we were advised to get as much sleep as we could. Dismas and Joe informed us that we would be starting our climb at midnight, and we would have our wake-up call at 11:15 PM. We learned that the teams would be leaving at staggered start times to avoid congesting the path. We had only one room in this camp; there were still many other dorms, and the various tents on the grounds had to be coordinated. We would be one of the last groups to leave our dorm. Starting at 9:00 PM, the other teams in our room would be woken in preparation for their hike. For a brief moment, we questioned

Dismas's decision and asked why we would be leaving so late. Wouldn't there be crowds to deal with by then? We had planned our summit time to be at sunrise. What if we missed it?

Dismas firmly reminded us that his lead was not to be questioned. This was now very serious business, and lives were held in the balance. We quickly and humbly retracted our questions. We had no more experience to successfully and safely summit Kilimanjaro than a first-time passenger would have in telling an airline pilot how to fly the plane. Returning to our dorms, we took another Diamox tablet and buried our heads deeply into our sleeping bags.

Sleep was a series of disconnected naps, as the first crew creaked open the wooden door and, with their bright headlights, roused their prospective teams. The drowsy hikers would then clumsily jump from their bunks and begin to layer up for their adventure. It was hard to keep nerves and excitement under control. One by one, each team left the room, ready to start their ascent. 11:15 PM could not come soon enough.

Finally, it was time for our call. With headlights beaming into the room, our guides quietly entered. They were followed by our cook who, to my surprise, placed our breakfast on the centre table. Breakfast had not been provided for the others who had left previously, so the sight of a pot of porridge, stacks of toast, plates of sausages, and metal carafes of tea was completely unexpected. Not wishing to test my stomach's newly acquired state of equilibrium, I went again for my comfort food. I had never been a fan of porridge in the past, but it had become a staple on this adventure.

Moments later, dressed and packed with water and energy bars, we stood at our meeting point away from the building, close to the steep incline that we were about to tackle. Dismas gave us our marching orders, and one by one we followed our leader into the darkness. The chilling temperature had dropped significantly as our breath hovered motionlessly in the air. The stillness was deceiving, as our position at the base camp had sheltered us from the impeding winds we would soon face. I had placed Hot Paws strips on my feet, hands, and back in an effort to make the most out of my clothing layers. This would be the warmest we were going to be for the next six hours, so staying alert and positive would be our challenge.

Dismas led us with a slow and rhythmic gait. As this was the steepest incline of the mountain, we would be traversing the gradient in a switchback formation. It was the safest way to move up the steep, 1,000-meter (3,280-foot) path in the course of six hours. The terrain was not only steep but had also changed significantly, challenging a nighttime maneuver. The upper portion of the mountain consisted of large boulders and rocks, mixed with loose scree, which could shift and roll at any time.

Within minutes of our mesmerizingly slow pace, we heard what sounded like cheers. We immediately thought that a team ahead of us had made it to the top and were cheering. But Dismas stopped and listened intently. Then we heard it. A few loose rocks and dirt rumbled down on the path behind us. A common occurrence and cause of injury was the potential of rockslides. Deaths had been noted with climbers being hit by falling and rolling rocks. The shouts we had heard were not those of cheers but of warning.

Our first break was about 30 minutes into the climb. We were all feeling pretty good but thankful for the stop. The altitude had made our feet feel like lead. The walk was slow, but none of us were interested in challenging Dismas's pace.

I reached for my drinking tube, which was attached to my water pack. Something was wrong. I turned the nozzle to the open position and waited for the flow, but nothing happened. Joe noticed that I was struggling and identified the reason my water was not flowing: My tube was frozen, stopping the water flow. Only 30 minutes in, and my water supply was turning into a giant ice cube! This was problematic, as I needed hydration.

It was time to improvise. Quickly removing my coat and pack, I repositioned the tube and the pack so that my body would keep the water from freezing completely. Removing my coat was not ideal as we were now beginning to feel the mountain's cold winds. The good news was that, once my coat was on, I could warm up my water with my body heat and continue to drink along the way. The bad news was that my body was now chilled, and conserving body heat was paramount.

We knew that we had many hours yet to climb, and my hands and face were growing numb from the freezing wind and dropping temperatures. Looking up still offered no sense that we were making progress. But we had read that, if you could get to Gilman's Point—the first major landmark on the way to Uhuru—then we would make it all the way. This part of the climb was without a doubt the most difficult—if not physically, most definitely mentally. The wind and temperatures continued to batter us, while our legs grew heavier with each footstep. It was most disconcerting when we would make way for climbers doubling back, unable to make it to the top. We watched as their guides helped their weak bodies down the mountain, reminding us that what was ahead was not going to get easier.

Sensing our somber mood and our focus slipping away, Dismas allowed a slightly longer break than our typical 30-second stop. Due to the dangers of the temperature and the reduced oxygen supply, taking longer breaks was dangerous. But Dismas took a chance. He turned to us and started to sing, "Don't Worry, Be Happy." It was the change we needed—the proverbial shot in the arm, so to speak. With a new song running through my head, we continued with the mantra, "Just get to Gilman's. Just get to Gilman's."

Our mood was positive, but we were undeniably weary. Our only sense of progress came from looking down, where a winding string of glimmering headlights from the hikers far below slithered in the distance, maneuvering the switchbacks over the winding paths. Looking up reminded us that Gilman's Point was still out of sight.

We had been on the trail for over four hours, climbing over boulders and shimmying past sheer-faced edges. So far, the physical requirements were well within my capabilities. But, through the rhythmic motion of our pace, I let my mind go numb, putting me in serious danger. Instead of remaining alert and aware of my surroundings, I allowed myself to fall into a trancelike *state and moved my left foot forward and shuffled my right. That was soon a dangerous choice as the toe of my right boot had not cleared a jagged rock and became tightly lodged, catapulting my entire body forward. From the waist up, I had plummeted over the edge of the mountain, hanging over a dark abyss, my boot holding firmly in place.*

Seconds later, Cam quickly pulled me up and brought me back to my feet. That close call was a reminder to never become complacent. Allowing the routine of the moment to mesmerize me was an error I would not repeat. When we become desensitized due to mind-numbing sameness, we run the risk of missing critical changes around us. We had come so far, and this was a dangerous lapse of awareness. From that point on, I was determined to be completely present, every step of the way.

Rounding a corner of yet another switchback, a shining beacon came out of nowhere, heralding Gilman's Point at 5,685 meters (18,652 feet). Any doubts that we may have allowed along the journey had dissipated. We had made Gilman's Point and, if our calculations were correct, we would be less than one hour away from Uhuru.

Gilman's Point provided a flatter plateau where people were resting before they continued. Dismas maintained his pace and guided us past the resting climbers, some of whom were making the dangerous decision to close their eyes. The temperatures and wind were relentless at this elevation. Sleepiness was a sign of severe altitude sickness. The best thing to do at this point was to keep moving. There would be more than enough opportunity to sleep later. For now, we had to keep our momentum.

Twenty minutes later, we had made it to Stella Point at 5,756 meters (18,885 feet). We were moments away from the goal that we had come half a world away to achieve. Our mood was contagiously spirited, and we were full of renewed excitement. I was so focused on the reality of standing on the top of Uhuru that I was unaware of a lack of feeling in my feet, hands, and face.

Then the excitement gained momentum. With only meters ahead, we could make out the monument that stated, "Congratulations! You are now at Uhuru Peak, Tanzania, 5895M. AMSL. Africa's Highest Point. World's Highest Free-Standing Mountain. One of the World's Largest Volcanoes. WELCOME." The exhilaration of seeing our goal just steps ahead of us was surreal. The fact that the temperature had dropped to -21 degrees C (-6 degrees F), not counting a strong wind chill, was not registering. As our team approached the monumental sign, we attempted to retrieve our cameras from deep in our layered clothing. Joe had to help me unzip my coat to retrieve my camera, as I had no feeling in my hands for such intricate maneuvers.

The photos would not capture the ultimate joy we felt when we reached Uhuru Peak. Clearly we were not models prepping for a photo shoot. The photos would however show the frozen strains of taking on a goal that was outside of our comfort level, adapting to the challenges of maneuvering the many obstacles and the ultimate result of successfully conquering the mountain.

Taking in the view from our newly experienced vantage was perfectly timed, as we silently watched the awakening of a new day. A most spectacular sunrise was cresting in the eastern horizon. Despite the challenges and obstacles, we had done it! Believing that action makes traction, we knew that this experience would be the stepping stone for yet another goal, another proverbial mountain. But before that next goal was to be decided, we would take in the moment to feel on top of the world.

The only thing better than successfully achieving your goals is to celebrate with the team that made it happen!

A.C.T.I.O.**N.** PLAN

How to Create the Next Phase for Your Business

You have probably picked up on the theme that success is based on action. I have shared the fundamental steps required to prepare you and your business for sustainable success.

You have discovered the importance of the Awareness phase as you evaluate:

- Your unique skills, experiences, and passions, and how they can be utilized in your business; and
- Your business purpose and its target market.

We have examined the importance of:

- Being clearly committed to your business venture; and
- Generating enthusiasm, which is transferred to those who will support your business from investors and staff to potential clients.

From there, you established whom you needed to support your venture by:

- Evaluating your current team or, if you were starting at the beginning, the team you need to find; and
- Examining the four pillars (visionary, strategist, implementer, and evaluator), who were set to support your plan.

As the team began to move in unison toward a common goal, strategies and KPIs were formulated, instigated, evaluated, and tweaked. The W.I.N. Model challenged you to evaluate what your business was showcasing and how to develop and grow your client base. This Implementation phase initiated traction that started to build momentum.

In our last chapter, you were introduced to the concept of acting on and creating your own opportunities. This phase showed you how getting away from working "in the business," in order to experience fresh new concepts, was critical for your own health and the health of your business.

Each of these steps is presented in a logical progression. As I mentioned at the beginning of this book, it is not necessary to achieve perfection. In fact, don't even try. Perfection is impossible to define in a changing world. The word "perfection" intimates a place of completeness; a stage of confirmed finality, suggesting no need to adjust. I cannot think of a successful business, small or large, that is not in a state of change.

In order to keep your business successfully building traction, we enter the next phase of the A.C.T.I.O.N. Plan and, by no sheer coincidence, "N" stands for Next. It is not the final stage in the A.C.T.I.O.N. Plan strategy but the continuum of what is to follow. This allows you to evaluate all that you have done so far. Engaging in the Next phase can take years, depending on whether you are starting your business venture from the beginning or fine-tuning an existing operation. Once you have reached it, you can step back and look at what you have accomplished … so far.

A ball will balance on the tip of a finger only when it is in motion. Motion keeps your business in the game.

Now What?

Are we there yet? Evaluating your current business status should not be a foreign concept at this point. Gain a broad perspective of how your business is progressing by obtaining feedback from your team and your clients.

Climb Your Mountain

Obtain quarterly and annual business evaluations by staff and clients to gain insight about how to move your business forward. Check out on-line, 360-degree evaluation templates to allow staff anonymous feedback on the business. On-line questionnaires can be developed for client feedback. These can be included in a customer service package that allows for anonymous comments. Receiving information through internal channels allows your business to deal with situations as they occur, rather than experiencing a besmirched client's comment on the Internet.

Remember: You are gathering facts to make informed decisions. These evaluations should not elicit tension.

Look at your current results, and compare them to the expected goals and KPIs. Some results to evaluate include:

✓ Revenue targets: _____

_____

✓ Department goals:_____

_____

✓ Cost projections: _____

_____

✓ Profit-and-loss statements (compare monthly and year to date):_____

_____

✓ Staffing and training goals:_____

_____

✓ Client growth and maintenance goals: _____

_____

✓ Marketing goals: _____

_____

✓ Systems or operational goals (process development or equipment upgrades): _____

_____

✓ Personal goals for both you and your team: _____

_____

Obtain the information in an easy-to-retrieve-and-review format. A member of your Implementation pillar would likely have the skills to create charts and graphs that can be easily reviewed by your entire team.

Monthly increments are helpful to identify trends and seasonal effects. Notes during the business seasons are helpful in order to explain the results (e.g., "Blizzard in first week of January resulted in power outage for 2 days; office closed" or "City won bid for Olympics; product demand for month of July increased by 87%"). These blips or anomalies need to be put into perspective so you do not assume the following January or July will experience the same results.

Big-Picture View

Start with big-picture statistics, and support them with detailed reports. For example, sales results could be observed with the following data:

- Total sales for all departments
- Individual department sales
- Results by salesperson
- Product and service breakdown

Run these results on monthly, quarterly, and total year-to-date bases, and compare the same to previous years. When you see results from different angles, you can identify trends and anomalies more easily. Let's say revenue was on target but, when you reviewed the department details, you identified three areas that were soaring with one underperforming.

Without this detailed analysis, this underperformance might go unnoticed, yet this area needs attention.

Your stats may also uncover any potential bottlenecks in your business. Perhaps your results show that, although your sales team is attracting qualified customers, the clients don't stay due to backlog on product delivery. This may result in identifying the need to hire and train staff in a particular area due to natural growth of your business; perhaps you require a Plan B if you identify that your bottleneck is supplier-based.

These are some of the results to watch for as your business develops and grows. Other areas include real expenditures compared to budgeted costs, hiring and training practices compared to staffing goals, and achieved market share compared to projected targets. Ultimately you want to look at any statistic that will give you a clear picture of how your business is performing.

Request detailed reports, and compare the results to the projected goals to make effective decisions regarding the Next phase of your business.

Remember: Knowledge is king in business, and details provide the signs you need to evaluate in order to act with agility.

Choosing Your Path

When you routinely evaluate the progress of your business, you will be faced with three distinct paths:

1. Your results indicate progress toward your goal, implying that your processes and strategies are working as expected. With minor adjustments, you can anticipate that your business is on track to meet its goals. Review monthly with a broad check at the next quarter.

2. You are not making the progress you expected. Detailed reports should provide the puzzle piece to help you identify what is

missing. Go back through the previous five steps and identify what needs attention.

Knowledge is king in business.

- Was there something missing in the Awareness phase? Were you "blindsided"? Did you miss a sign along the way that set you back?
- Did you waiver in your commitment to clearly define what you do and who your client is? Did your team share your vision? Did you take on clients or projects that your gut said you shouldn't have?
- Do you have the right number of the right people doing the right tasks in your business? Are your four pillars represented effectively for the stage of your business?
- Review your Implementation and Opportunities strategies. What might you have missed?

Once you have identified the missing piece, return to that phase, make the corrections, and move on. Ensure that you determine a timeline to make this correction and monitor closely.

3. If you are looking down this next path, start the fireworks! Your diligence has paid off as your business has achieved the goals you had intended. It may take time for your goals to be realized; however, as you achieve all of your KPIs (see "Develop Strong

*It never stops.
The A.C.T.I.O.N.
Plan is
perpetual.*

KPIs" on page 116 in the Implementation phase) and benchmarks, you will find that you are now positioned to be a contender to lead your industry.

So now what?

Remember: The "N" stands for Next—the sixth stage is not the last because the process is perpetual. Once you have accomplished your goals, the momentum of your business signals the beginning for a new A.C.T.I.O.N. Plan sequence.

If you are standing on the summit of your goal, then you are ready to embark on a new journey, which takes us right back to beginning of the A.C.T.I.O.N. Plan. Ensure the areas that require maintenance are maintained, and start to focus on *new* goals. Those new goals will lead you right back to the Awareness phase. You know so much more than you did when you first started; now use that knowledge to propel you to your next targets.

Review and adjust your commitment and your mission to reflect the new venture. Evaluate and adjust your team to adequately support your new endeavours. Design and initiate effective strategies to be implemented and monitored in order to determine whether you are progressing as intended, and build on the opportunities that you have created.

What might that look like in the real world?

Perhaps you will decide that, once you have achieved your business goals, you are ready to expand and franchise your business or open additional businesses in other cities. These are all new ventures with a completely different path than your original one. By applying the A.C.T.I.O.N. Plan to your new ventures, you can ensure that you have an effective map to guide you to your new summit.

Every goal you reach becomes your foundation for the next!

One More Thing ...

Business owners often neglect to establish an exit strategy. It is critical to consider when and how to exit your business. To ensure that you are building toward your legacy, ask yourself:

- How long do I want to run this business?
- Who can take over if I am incapacitated?
- How would I sell my business?
- How do I determine what my business is worth?
- What if I want to leave it to my family?
- Should I create a board of directors?

Just as you have a plan for the success of your business, you need to consider your plan for succession. If you and your team embrace the A.C.T.I.O.N. Plan, the baton of your legacy will ripple into generations to come.

In Summary

The "N" phase of the A.C.T.I.O.N. Plan asks the question, "What will you do next?" It represents the culmination of all the stages, but it is never considered an ending. The A.C.T.I.O.N. Plan is perpetual, thus the name. Business owners who are successful know how important it is to continuously learn, evaluate, and act in order to maintain momentum toward achieving goals.

We also know that, if we do not allow ourselves checkpoints along the way, we run the risk of getting off course. The Next phase helps you assess your progress by providing three options for your continued course of action. The process builds on the knowledge, experience, and success garnered from each stage.

1. You are progressing toward your goals as expected and will continue to follow your strategies until you meet your goals satisfactorily.

2. You are not meeting your targets as you had anticipated. Review the previous stages and identify where you need to make a correction before you continue.

3. You have successfully completed your goals and are ready for a new plan. Perhaps you wish to expand, diversify, or prepare for succession. All of these goals represent a new chapter, which means starting the A.C.T.I.O.N. Plan back at the Awareness phase.

Success is a process that requires traction,
and traction is achieved with A.C.T.I.O.N.

*May this A.C.T.I.O.N. Plan serve to guide
your business to sustainable success.*

May success be yours.

*Today is a blank page. What will you
write on it at the end of the day?*

Sunrise view from Mount Kilimanjaro's summit, Uhuru Peak.

Next Business Strategy

Next Interview with Rob Petkau

https://goo.gl/kSbxxC
(time 10:30)

https://goo.gl/CHj5eE
(time 19:34)

Using a scan app, scan the QR code above, or use
the above link to access the sound file.

Note: Please allow a few moments for the file to open on your device.

A.C.T.I.O.N. PLAN

APPENDIX A

Step-by-Step
Business Plan

Cover Page: **Company name**
                     Contact information
                     Date

Table of Contents (include page numbers)

A. Executive Summary
B. Business Profile
C. Ownership and Management Structure
D. Business Environment
E. Goals and Objectives
F. Marketing Plan
G. Operations
H. Financial Statements
I. Financial Requirements
J. Exit Strategy
K. Appendix

A. Executive Summary

An overview of the key points of the business plan

Note: This is not a duplication of the points that follow. This is a summary of your entire business plan; therefore, although it is presented at the beginning for the intended reader, it must be prepared at the end of your research and preparation. The points that follow the executive summary will be succinct elaborations on the points mentioned.

The purpose of the business plan may be included if presented for a specific intent.

- **Business profile**
  - A brief history/description of your business, the industry, and the targeted market you intend to serve (see "Focus Your Business by Creating a Mission Statement" on page 62 for a concise statement)

- Description of products and services offered
- **Purpose of your business plan:** For example, the purpose may be to secure financing or to attract potential management team members or collaboration with other business opportunities.
- **Ownership and management structure:** Your business's legal description (e.g., sole proprietorship or corporation), summary of management titles and credentials, and advisor requirements.
- **Business environment:** Stage of your business, stage of the industry cycle, and growth anticipations. A brief analysis of your advantages and vulnerable areas and your plan to overcome these challenges.
- **Key initiatives and objectives**
  - Primary objectives for the first year
  - Future objectives
- **Marketing opportunities:** Present your target market description: who is your target market, where will you find them, and how will they find you? Provide a description of industry competition, business's competitive advantage, vulnerable areas, and plans to overcome them.
- **Operations:** An overview of locations, departments, staffing, and equipment/supplies required.
- **Financial requirements and forecasts:** Description of forecasts and how you established them. Specify financial requirements that are being requested and include brief descriptions of repayment timelines.

B. Business Profile

A description of the industry your business will be engaged in, including its purpose, physical presence, products, and services

Legal registered name: _____

_____

Trade name (if different from above): _____

_____

Contact information:

Business owner's name: _____

Your position: _____

Address: _____

_____

Mailing address (if different from above): _____

_____

Phone number: _____

Cell phone number: _____

FAX number: _____

Email: _____

Website: _____

Date business was established: _____

This business is:

❏ Newly established   ❏ Restructuring

❏ Currently existing   ❏ Expanding

Business ownership status:

❏ Sole proprietorship   Date of registration: _____

❏ Partnership   Date of registration: _____

❏ Corporation   Date of incorporation:_____

Industry sector (e.g., retail, manufacturing, or service):

State your industry and describe where that industry is in its life cycle.

Is there room for growth? _____

_____

Purpose of business (see "Focus Your Business by Creating a Mission Statement" on page 62): _____

_____

_____

Products and services provided (describe in detail and include how your business fulfills a need): _____

_____

C. Ownership and Management Structure

A description of who has decision-making abilities in your business as well as who is responsible for specific roles and activities

Note: Even if you do not currently have people fulfilling these roles, include a job description as it shows that you have thought through the direction your business is taking. This will be advantageous when you begin to attract people who are interested in your business. You will be able to hire according to your objectives.

- List the owners of the business, their roles, and percentage of ownership they have in the business (add job descriptions and resumes to the Appendix of this plan): _____

  _____

  _____

- List the departments in the company and the management or advisors assigned to each department (e.g., manufacturing, sales, administration, customer service, information technology, marketing, and human resources) (see the Appendix of this plan for the organizational chart): _____

  _____

- List the management team, their roles, and a short biography of each (add job descriptions and resumes to the Appendix of this plan): __

  _____

  _____

- If your company has a board of directors or advisors, list them here and include a short biography of each (add roles and resumes to the Appendix): _____

  _____

- Professional services (add all contact information to the Appendix). Bookkeeper: _____

  _____

  Accountant: _____

  _____

  Lawyer: _____

  _____

  Banker: _____

  _____

  Consultants: _____

  _____

D. Business Environment

A descriptor of your business's viability in a given industry including the life stage of the business and its ability to grow and maneuver challenges

If your business is currently operating, provide a history of its activities from the start date and include any sales, marketing, or staffing progress. Describe the industry that your business falls into. The following represents some areas to consider:

- Is this a well-established industry?
- Is there growth potential?
- Who is your competition in this industry?
- Who influences this industry?
- What are the long-term considerations for this industry?
- Does this industry experience seasonal factors?

- Are there economic factors that may affect this industry (e.g., interest rates)?
- Are there governmental considerations for this industry (e.g., interprovisional regulations or importing rules)?
- Is the industry influenced by trends or social concerns (e.g., reducing carbon footprint)?
- Is technology expanding or limiting this industry?

State your business's position in this industry:
- What are your business's advantages?
- How are you able to ensure a strong placement in the existing marketplace?
- What are the vulnerable spots in your business (e.g., products, services)?
- How are your services/products unique?
- Do you have your intellectual property protected via patent, copyright, or trademark?
- How easy can your business be duplicated and therefore be less unique?
- Do you have the credentials required for the industry requirements?

E.　Goals and Objectives

Specific goals presented as an achievable roadmap supported by relevant objectives

- **Goals** are broad descriptors of *what* you intend to achieve. They should tie to your mission statement. Your business goal or goals are what your business is about (i.e., why it exists).
- **Objectives** are the *how* required to achieve the specific goal. They provide the measurable processes that support progress toward the success of the goals.

Note: See the Implementation section for more details.

F. Marketing Plan

A plan that will position your business in a given industry, establish a growing client base, and secure anticipated market share

Define your target market and market share

- Identify your target market (i.e., describe the demographics): ____

  _____

- What is the size of the current market? _____

  _____

- What share of this market do you anticipate owning? What percentage do your competitors own? _____

  _____

Analysis of business position

- Provide results from a SWOT (Strengths/Weaknesses/ Opportunities/Threats) analysis (see page 111): _____

  _____

Competitors

- Who are your competitors? _____

  _____

- What are their strengths and weaknesses? _____

  _____

- How does your competition threaten your business? _____

  _____

Your competitive edge

- Why would clients choose your product or service? _____

  _____

- What is unique about your business's offerings? _____

  _____

- How do your products and services meet the needs of clients now and in the future? _____

  _____

- Do you have your intellectual property protected with trademarks, copyrights, licenses, or guarantees? _____

  _____

Note: Always get professional (e.g., legal, financial/accounting) assistance regarding protecting intellectual property. Never create an agreement without professional guidance.

Market research (attach any relevant research to the Appendix). Trends noted:

- What has been going on in the world, the industry, and the local marketplace that may impact clients' choices? _____

  _____

- Describe how you plan to address these trends as strengths to attaining future market shares: _____

  _____

- Do seasons impact your consumer base? How will you address this?

  _____

- How do you plan to attract clients? _____

  _____

- Describe your advertising plan (e.g., website, radio, print, mail):

  _____

- How will you distribute your products or services (e.g., direct, retail, wholesale, mail, online)? _____

  _____

G. Operations

An overview of how the business will run including physical space, staff, manufacturing process/product or service offerings, suppliers, and customer service

Location

Address: _____

_____

Space size (e.g., office, retail, manufacturing space, warehouse): _____

_____

Lease terms: _____

_____

Equipment

- List items: _____

  _____

- Indicate owned or leased: _____

  _____

- Indicate what you have and what you need: _____

  _____

Suppliers

- Suppliers (preferably with letters indicating business intent; add to the Appendix): _____

  _____

- Suppliers you intend to include in the future: _____

  _____

- Options for secondary supply sources, if required: _____

  _____

- Payment terms imposed by suppliers (add to the Appendix): _____

  _____

Cost centres

- Overhead costs (add any documents to the Appendix): _____

  _____

  _____

- Costs for products and services (add supporting documentation to the Appendix): _____

  _____

  _____

- How do you manage your inventory? _____

  _____

  _____

- What does your inventory cost to maintain? _____

  _____

  _____

Human resources

- Indicate full-time, part-time, and contract employees and their respective wages: _____

  _____

  _____

- Create a table to show expected staffing for first, second, and third years of operation: _____

  _____

  _____

Customer service

- How will you handle customer complaints and returns? _____

  _____

- Include any documents to the Appendix regarding warranty or guarantees. _____

  _____

Note: Ensure that professionals have reviewed such documents prior to utilizing them.

H. Financial Statements

A detailed representation of current financial activity as well as projected forecasts as presented in three key areas: balance sheet, income statement, and cash flow

Balance sheet: If business exists, provide yearly information for the past five years.

- Provide information in the following format (day/month/year) consistently and indicate the format at the beginning of the documents.

ASSETS	LIABILITIES AND SHAREHOLDER EQUITY
Current Assets	**Current Liabilities**
Cash	Short-term bank debt
Accounts Receivable	**Accounts Payable**
Inventory	Taxes
Prepaid expenses	
	Long-term debt:
Other:	Other:
Total Current Assets:	**Total Current Liabilities:**
Fixed Assets	**Long-term Liabilities**
Land	Long-term debt
Buildings	Other:

ASSETS	LIABILITIES AND SHAREHOLDER EQUITY
Equipment	
(Subtract accumulated depreciation)	
Total Fixed Assets:	**Total Long-term Liabilities:**
Intangible assets	Shareholder equity
Goodwill	Cash equity contribution
Patents	Stocks or shares
Trademarks	Retained earnings
Other:	**Total shareholder equity:**
Total Intangible Assets:	**Total Liabilities and Shareholder Equity:**
Total Assets:	

Income statement: If your business has been established for some time, use your previous year's data as a baseline, and then project your estimated future income for the next three years. If you are starting up a business venture, use this format to estimate what your first-, second-, and third-year income will be. Prepare forecasts on a quarterly basis.

Revenue or sales
Subtract Cost of Goods Sold (COGS)
Gross profit margin
Subtract:
Selling expenses
Office expenses

Payroll expenses
Interest expenses
Other or general expenses
Total operating expenses
Operating profit
Subtract:
Business taxes payable
Depreciation/amortization
Other
Subtotal
Net income

Cash flow: This represents cash (in) receivables and (out) payables over a period of time.

Cash flow forecast projected for 12 months (day, month, year)
Cash receipts
Cash from sales
Current month
Accounts receivable from previous month
Cash equity/debt contribution
Other cash received
Total cash receipts

Cash disbursements
Equipment purchases, rentals, down payments, or leases
Rent
Salaries
General staff
Management
Materials
Inventory
Marketing and promotion
Bank interest
General and admin expenses
Long-term debt payment (principal)
Taxes
Other
Total cash disbursements
Opening cash position
Monthly surplus or deficit
Closing cash position

I. Financial Requirements

Specific funding requirements, which must be obtained from a secondary source that you are responsible to manage and repay

- How much of your own funds do you have invested in your business to date? _____

  _____

  _____

- What additional funding plans to you have? _____

  _____

  _____

- Describe the details of these other fund sources: _____

  _____

  _____

- How many adjustments have you demonstrated to ensure that the business is running efficiently and is as lean as possible (only request what you absolutely need)? _____

  _____

  _____

- List how much money you require to run your business:
  - Monthly: _____
  - Quarterly: _____
  - Annually: _____
- How much do you need to borrow or attract as equity to meet these requirements? _____

  _____

- What are your borrowing/equity options?
  - Line of credit: _____
  - Mortgage: _____
  - Business loan: _____
  - Equipment loan: _____
  - Angel investors: _____
  - Other equity/loan: _____
- How will the funds be allocated (be specific)? _____

  _____

- Prepare a repayment schedule (i.e., amount and date): _____

  _____

- What collateral can you offer to support debt? _____

  _____

Current banking information

- Name of financial institution: _____

  _____

- Branch address: _____

  _____

- Accounts: _____

  _____

- List of loans available and outstanding: _____

  _____

- Repayment history: _____

  _____

J. Exit Strategy

Strategy your business intends to follow when the exit phase has been reached, and how the phase will be carried out per specific requirements

- Acquisition or merger
- Initial public offering (less likely for small business but possibly a consideration for franchise owners and larger operations)
- Internal buyout (such as employee or management)
- Family succession (if selected, requires a plan to ensure training for transition)
- Liquidation/dissolution

K. Appendix

A compilation of documents or reference material to clarify or support your business case

In addition to the information suggested, the following may be beneficial:

- Letters of credit or reference
- Current leases, showing up-to-date payments
- Contracts/agreements being honoured in good faith

- Letters of intent from potential clients
- Legal agreements

Appendix A Notes

As you begin to formulate your business plan, the topic of capital requirements will likely surface. Often, businesses need some form of capital to get things going. It can take years to start seeing a profit, so you need to have a secure financial plan in place. Meet with your bank manager/accountant to obtain advice on your best course of action.

Here are some financial options to consider:

- Small business bank loans
- Grants
- Venture capital
- Angel investors
- Partnerships

A.C.T.I.O.N. PLAN

A P P E N D I X   B

Learn the Lingo

Accounts payable: Combination of all money owed by the company to vendors or creditors for products or services used by the company that have been acquired on credit.

Accounts receivable: The combination of money owed to the company by clients for products and services provided.

Accumulated depreciation: The calculated deduction or depreciated value over time for assets such as buildings, vehicles, machinery, office equipment, furniture, and fixtures.

A.C.T.I.O.N. Plan: A process that moves individuals and businesses through the phases of Awareness, Commitment, Team, Implementation, Opportunities, and Next.

Assets: A resource with future economic value, which a business owns.

Balance sheet: The financial statement that shows the financial position of your business at a point in time, generally consisting of three parts: assets, liabilities, and owner's equity and capital.

Business culture: The unique set of values and behaviors that contribute to the working environment of an organization.

Business plan: A written document that explains how a business is going to achieve its goals, highlighting specific segments including marketing, financial, and operational activities.

Copyright: The exclusive and legal rights provided to the originator of materials related to print, publishing, performance, film, audio recordings, literary, artistic, or musical creations, all of which require others to obtain permission for use.

Cost of goods sold (COGS): Reflects direct costs associated with the final product or service that is sold, including the materials and labour required to create the product or service.

Demographics: Relates to the statistics of a specific subgroup in a given population sample.

Earnings before interest and taxes (EBIT): A measure of the business's operating profit including all expenses except interest and income tax expenses.

Entrepreneur: A person who is often involved in the inception, organization, and management of an enterprise or business, and is usually responsible for its initiative and risk.

Exit strategy: The planned exit of the owner. Planning for it, when developing the business plan, is recommended with adjustments over time. This strategy takes into consideration when and how you want to exit or transition your business. This may include planning to establish a board of advisors/directors to ensure the continuation of your company, even if you are no longer making the key decisions. By having a clear mission and business plan, a board of advisors/directors can act on your behalf as you set up the process. Other strategies to consider, if you intend to pass the business to family members over time, are determining the key roles and responsibilities in advance to ensure the potential candidates have time to develop into the roles. You may find that your intent is to franchise or sell your business. These paths require specific action steps to ensure that you strengthen your brand and maximize your profit potential. All of these steps need to be planned in advance and will require the advice from trusted sources.

Gross margin: Sales – cost of sales.

Gross margin (percentage): Calculated by taking the company's total sales revenue, minus the COGS, and then dividing by the total sales revenue. (Multiplying by 100 will allow you to express the value as a percentage: gross margin (%) = revenue – COGS/revenue x 100.) A company that produces high margin ratios has more money to pay operating expenses, such as salaries, rent, and utilities.

Gross revenue: Accounts for all income from a sale. If a company pays commission to their sales team, then net revenue may be reported.

Income statement: Measures your company's performance from operating activities for a specific accounting/time period (sometimes referred to as a "profit and loss statement"). It indicates both revenues and expenses from operating activities. It will indicate a net profit or loss of a specific accounting period being analyzed.

Investor: An individual who provides capital with the expectations of a future financial reward/return. It may be offered in the form of currency, real estate, equity, commodity, or debt securities.

Key Performance Indicators (KPIs): Established, measurable values that allow a business to monitor progress toward goals. An effective KPI follows the SMART goal protocol (Specific, Measurable, Achievable, Relevant, and Time).

Liabilities: The financial debt that is accumulated in the course of running a business with the anticipation of settling payment in the future.

Mission statement: Reflects the vision and values of the company, which allows the business team and potential clients to understand the business fundamentally.

Net income/profit: Also called "net earnings," and informally "the bottom line." The business revenue – the business expenses (the cost of goods sold + expenses) for a specific accounting period. May be before or after taxes.

Objectives: Like goals, objectives are actions that support the overall endeavours of the purpose of your business. Where a goal is broader, an objective is more specific and can be supported by measurable activities and KPIs.

Operating profit: The earnings before interest and taxes.

Retained earnings: Refers to the accumulated after-tax profits earned to date, minus any dividends or distributions made to investors.

Revenue: The amount of money that a company receives before any deductions are applied. It is the first item on a profit-and-loss statement from which all costs and expenses are deducted.

Search engine optimizers: Used to improve a website's placement in the World Wide Web kingdom. By using key words, effective search engine optimizers will help position your website to enable those looking for your services to find you with ease.

SMART: The acronym that refers to the five critical components of effective business goals (Specific, Measurable, Achievable, Relevant, and Time). Key Performance Indicators (KPIs) are used to measure performance in attaining these goals. Credit for creating this process has been given to George T. Doran (1981).

Strengths, Weaknesses, Opportunities, and Threats (SWOT) analysis: Analyzes a business in terms of its strengths, weaknesses, opportunities, and threats. While the strengths and weaknesses are an internal review, the opportunities and threats evaluate the industry and the bigger world in which the business exists. Albert Humphrey has been credited with the creation of the SWOT analysis during his research at Stanford University (1960-70), where he focused on developing an analytical tool that evaluated why corporate strategies succeeded as well as failed.

Venture capital: Money provided by investors for start-up businesses that show promise of growth with profit.

W.I.N. Model: The three steps to successful client development (Window Shopping, Ideal Client, and Networking).

A.C.T.I.O.N. PLAN

A P P E N D I X C

Downloadable
PDF Forms

———

Link for downloadable pdf forms:
https://goo.gl/An51uL

Business Evaluation Checklist

Business Inventory List

Define Your Client

Performance Review

Personal Inventory List

Reference Checklist

SWOT

The Business Plan

The W.I.N. Model Checklist

Your Future Business

Your Personal Awareness Questionnaire

About the Author

Leanne Brownoff is a business coach, strategy consultant, keynote speaker, and writer. She believes that business is best approached like a science experiment, where keen observation and curiosity can lead to results that surpass expectations. Her varied and eclectic career, business experiences, and travel opportunities have given her a great deal of insight on what it takes to make a business thrive in a globally changing world.

Leanne's career path has found her strategizing in boardrooms with key decision makers, training national teams, and inspiring innovative projects for large corporations as well as medium and small businesses. This expertise led her to the development of the A.C.T.I.O.N. Plan, a business model that has consistently guided business owners, entrepreneurs, and senior management to create a trusted roadmap that moves companies confidently through shifting and uncertain terrain.

Although she is busy with her career, sitting on advisory boards, regularly writing for the *Edmonton Journal,* and volunteering for many charities, she finds her balance by spending time with her family and enjoying the great outdoors. Her thirst for travel and the experiences it can bring has been fruitful but not without infamous notes: She has experienced a 7.6 earthquake, a government uprising on a tropical island, and the tragic events of September 11, 2001. She was once chided by a colleague, who said, "Remind me never to go traveling with you!" to which she replied, "I always come back with a memorable story!" Her latest travel experience was to take on Mount Kilimanjaro with her daughter.

This resulted in a touching experience that found her humbled by the Masai people and astounded at the immenseness of the mountain and its grandeur.

Leanne's inspiration comes from people who appreciate today yet eagerly anticipate the future. She believes firmly in doing what you love and leaving things better than you found them. Her motto is *"Don't be a spectator in your own life. You are intended to play the leading role. Do it with passion!"*

Contributor Bios

Rob Petkau

Genesis Coaching
(see "Chapter 1: Awareness" on page 31)

As an experienced professional coach with many years of experience, Rob has guided individuals on their quest to experience more fulfilling lives. His work with youth and adults has provided a vast arena in which to connect with individuals from all life stages, backgrounds, and interests. His work with entrepreneurs has been particularly impactful as his clients gain insight on both their personal and professional goals. As an entrepreneur, Rob understands the hunger of the artistic mind and the challenges of creating traction while juggling responsibilities with opportunities.

Dr. Deborah Nixon, PhD

(see "Chapter 2: Commitment" on page 51)

Dr. Deborah Nixon received her PhD in Organizational Development, focusing on trust and its impact on individuals and organizations. She offers consulting services to both public- and private-sector organizations in the areas of organizational development, change management, leadership development, human resources strategies, and strategic and business planning. Her strong background in marketing and advertising provides great insight to her clients who are experiencing change and requiring solid advice to help them commit to new processes and strategies. Her policy advice skills are coveted at the highest level of government. In addition to her big-picture vantage of business development, Deborah is a trained facilitator and certified to administer Hogan and McQuaig assessments, delivering leadership and team-building seminars and workshops across the country. Her goal is to focus her clients on being committed to developing high-trust relationships with both their teams and their clients.

Deborah's impressive and impactful career path started from humble beginnings when she was faced with an uncertain future as a young widow with a young son. Forced to manage her money and future, Deborah obtained her PhD in trust, studying wealth-management firms and their clients. She established a popular program, My Money Mindset, dedicated to helping women gain confidence in managing their money and therefore their future. Deborah is currently a managing director at Mandrake Human Capital. A regular contributor to the *Huffington Post* and a cycling enthusiast, Deborah is committed to living her life fully and shares her verve with everyone she meets.

Dale Monaghan

President and CEO, Goodwill Industries of Alberta
(see "Chapter 3: Team" on page 71)

When it comes to creating impactful results, Dale Monaghan knows the importance of leadership and developing a winning team. Dale has significant experience in both business and community development through years of service at the senior leadership level of Goodwill Industries of Alberta, the Mikisew Group of Companies, Alberta Legislature, City of Edmonton (Office of the Mayor), Travel Alberta, and the municipal government.

Dale's experience in business development and marketing at the national and international levels has provided opportunities to develop teams that execute bar-raising results. A graduate of the University of Alberta (Bachelor of Physical Education, specializing in organizational development and sports marketing) and the Queen's School of Business Executive Development Program, Dale is an active volunteer in the community, including serving on the board of directors of the 2012 Alberta Winter Games, helping with the Special Olympics, and coaching youth fastball. In order to balance his hectic schedule and responsibilities, Dale can be found enjoying his country home with his wife Laurella and daughter Becki.

Dianna Bowes

Creator of the Fabulous@50 Experience and Martini Party
Creative Editor of *Be Fabulous! Magazine*
Webmaster
http://www.fabulousat50.com
(see "Chapter 4: Implementation" on page 97)

Whether you meet Dianna Bowes face to face or hear her speak at an event, you are immediately captivated by her passion. Her story depicts a humble beginning as well as a series of devastating moments that defined her early life. Raised by her grandparents from birth, she observed her world through the lens of violence and addiction.

Marrying her high school sweetheart was a singularly joyful moment—only to have it ripped away when he tragically died 10 days before their first anniversary and before her 21st birthday. The following years were tumultuous, filled with abuse and despair. Buried deeply under the weight of pain, Dianna found the strength to redefine who she was and, rising through the despair of her existence, decided to channel her efforts to help women find their inner voice.

Seeing a need for women to safely discover their own paths and realize their most coveted dreams, Dianna established Fabulous@50. The program began as small groups of Baby Boomer-aged women gathered to network and bond on topics relating to health, career, family, travel, culture, and nutrition—in fact, any topic that was of interest. Dianna initiated the program through a series of carefully implemented steps.

Due to the popularity of the meetings, Dianna expanded her interests to include tradeshows, special events, and publications, making Fabulous@50 into a major brand. Now a published author of her book, *The Fabulous@50 Re-Experience: It's never too late to refresh your mind, body and spirit and you don't have to do it alone,* Dianna has developed her service into a licensed business, spreading the seeds of support to other communities.

MoJo Design Inc.

Owners Maureen Wright and Johanne Lewis
http://www.mojodesigninc.com
(see "Chapter 5: Opportunities" on page 143)

When one creative spark ignites the imagination, the result can be impressive; when two such sparks combine, the outcome can be spectacular. The latter was the case when innovative interior designers Maureen Wright and Johanne Lewis started working together at Ethan Allen. Unique in their talents and approach yet focused on a combined vision, they stood heads above others in their field. In February 2010, the two decided to combine their talents and, by blending the beginnings of each of their first names, started the design business MoJo Design Inc.

Maureen and Johanne moved through the challenges in the early years by using their creative, solution-oriented skills, seeking and creating opportunities that were hiding in everyday challenges. Moving their business into a highly visible area and participating in numerous community fundraising events garnered them regular appearances on television and in print. To keep up with public demand, their business grew from two to a team of five, as referred clients sought their talents to have their home "mojo'd."

As they connected with leading local and national artisans in the design business, they developed a platform to showcase this talent. In 2016, they completed their third annual Vignettes production. Spearheaded by MoJo team member Leigh Wright, MoJo Vignettes invites designers, artisans, and product suppliers to work in teams to create small-room masterpieces. The Vignettes are then judged and opened to the public for viewing.

In just over six years, MoJo Design Inc. has become synonymous with innovative solutions—whether working with individual clients or coordinating the artisan/design world in a spectacular event. Maureen Wright and Johanne Lewis design their business path by creating opportunities, which puts them in a league of their own.

Rob Petkau

Owner, Head Designer, Genesis Custom Sabers
https://genesiscustomsabers.com
(see "Chapter 6: Next" on page 169)

Being true to his coaching message, Rob listened to his own advice and followed his passion. When asked, he describes himself as an artist, but he creates for a very dedicated and particular niche: Rob is a designer and builder of real, dueling lightsabers. His designs and creations have garnered him top nods from some of the most hardcore critics, such as *Star Wars* enthusiasts and sci-fi fans. Since he first saw *Star Wars Episode V: The Empire Strikes Back* as a child, he dreamed of creating a working lightsaber. Now he runs a complete manufacturing business with clients all over the world. Rob is a consummate entrepreneur and is experienced in the challenges of creating a successful startup business while managing the important role of husband and father. His journey brings inspiration to those who dream of following their passion.

71018865R00128

Made in the USA
Middletown, DE
19 April 2018